FLAVOR x FIRE

DEREK WOLF

OVER THE FIRE
— COOKING —

Inspiring | Educating | Creating | Entertaining

Brimming with creative inspiration, how-to projects, and useful information to enrich your everyday life, quarto.com is a favorite destination for those pursuing their interests and passions.

First Published in 2022 by The Harvard Common Press, an imprint of The Quarto Group,
100 Cummings Center, Suite 265-D, Beverly, MA 01915, USA.
T (978) 282-9590 F (978) 283-2742 Quarto.com

The Harvard Common Press titles are also available at discount for retail, wholesale, promotional, and bulk purchase. For details, contact the Special Sales Manager by email at specialsales@quarto.com or by mail at The Quarto Group, Attn: Special Sales Manager, 100 Cummings Center, Suite 265-D, Beverly, MA 01915, USA.

26 25 24 23 22   1 2 3 4 5

ISBN: 978-0-7603-7493-1

Digital edition published in 2022
eISBN: 978-0-7603-7494-8

Library of Congress Cataloging-in-Publication Data available

Cover Design and page layout: Amy Sly
Photography: Jack Sorokin Photography; except page 9, which is courtesy of Maryland Public Television
Food Styling: Mackenzie Luttrell

Printed in China

DEDICATION
To my loving wife, Ally, you make every day full of wonder, joy, and excitement. I love you.

Recipes and Techniques for Bigger,
Bolder BBQ and Grilling

FLAVOR

x

FIRE

DEREK WOLF

OVER THE FIRE
— COOKING —

HARVARD
COMMON
PRESS

CONTENTS

FOREWORD

I first encountered Derek Wolf the way most people do: scrolling through social media posts.

Here was a guy who cooked in the most primal way possible: always outdoors, often in the woods, and, invariably over a blazing wood fire. He used primal tools: massive cleavers, forged knives, and skewers that look like pitchforks. He painted with bold flavors: garlic, chile peppers, cilantro, coffee. Often, he didn't even bother to cook on a grill grate.

His recipes were shockingly original, too: grilled chorizo rafts topped with pepperjack cheese and chimichurri. Towers of burgers roasted vertically on a trompo—to be carved onto flame seared tacos. (How's *that* for a twist on *tacos al pastor*.) Steak, egg, and asparagus breakfasts that would force Paul Bunyan to loosen his belt—cooked, you guessed it, over a wood fire.

Derek's camera work is as original as his food. Ingredients leaping into bowls or skillets. Assembled and grilled in a rush of staccato video. Ingenious grilling techniques, followed by a simple luscious bite, followed by Derek's signature gesture of delectation: a thumbs up.

After watching more than a few videos, I realized something impressive: each one lasted less than a minute but taught as much as you'd learn in an entire afternoon cooking class. And most amazing of all: he hadn't uttered a single word.

I quickly became hooked and realized I certainly wasn't alone. In just a few years, Derek had acquired millions of followers online across his various Over The Fire Cooking accounts. Whether it's his photos or videos, people can't get enough of him, and neither can I.

His culinary accomplishments are all the more remarkable for the fact that he is completely self-taught, which brings me in a roundabout way to his handsome new book: *Flavor by Fire*. And, man, what a book! Chock-a-block full of the sort of big flavor, in-your-face food that has made Derek such a social media phenomenon. You'll find hanging monster beef tomahawks grilled vertically over a smoky wood fire; honey habanero rotisserie turkey; baked lobster with buffalo chive butter; garlic parmesan beer chicken legs; chipotle mezcal smoked shrimp. The recipe titles read like poetry, each dish more stunning and expertly charred than the next. It's a wonder you don't lick the pages.

Some months ago, intrigued by Derek's singular videos and books, I invited him to be a guest on my *Project Fire* television show. In the back of my mind, I wondered: How would this master griller—so brilliant on social media—perform on live television? Would he be like some of the silent movie stars of yore: compelling without words, but lost with the advent of talkies? Well, as you may have seen in *Project Fire*, Derek is every bit as articulate live and *in voce viva*, as he is on social media and in his books.

If you love the thrill of grilling over live fire, you'll want this book. If you hunger for creative flavor combinations and food that fairly screams in your mouth, you need this book. If you're aiming to reproduce Derek Wolf's masterpieces on your own grill, well, just study this book, because this social media star turns out to be one hell of a writer, too.

—Steven Raichlen
Miami, Florida

INTRODUCTION

"If I had one wish, I would want to watch my favorite movie again for the first time."
—Unknown movie critic

The first time I cooked over a live fire, I made skirt steaks cooked right over the hot coals, with a homemade chimichurri sauce, green beans, and potatoes. It was a simple meal, but sitting next to my wife at the table, I will never forget the look of amazement on her face (and, I'm sure, on mine as well). We had never experienced these flavors before. I think I made that recipe three or four more times just that next week because I couldn't get enough! The memory of the hot fire, sizzling steaks, and enjoying that dinner together will stay with me forever. That cook made me realize that the flavor from the fire leaves a lasting impression.

So, here we are today! After hundreds of recipes on my blog and socials, and an entire book devoted to cooking over fire, I find myself more interested in flavor than ever. My belief is that you do not need complex ingredients cooked on insanely expensive grills to make really good food. Yes, this book might have a few exceptions here and there, such as Wild Sage and Cranberry Venison Rack (page 183), Spicy Hoisin Jerk Rotisserie Duck (page 198), and Black Garlic New York Strips with Bone Marrow Butter (page 69), but in those cases the extra effort is worth it. (And, I know my readers were born ready!)

The mission of this cookbook is the marriage of flavor and fire—using flavor to spice up your grill and utilizing fire to make showstopping meals. Whereas my first book, *Food by Fire*, focused on classic fire cooking techniques to build a good foundation for grilling, this book, *Flavor by Fire*, dives deep into amplifying the flavors of food, to help the backyard cook better understand, harness, and enhance the power of flavor through approachable recipes using easily sourced ingredients that deliver delicious results. Ultimately, I want you to experience moments like I have had, creating memories with family and friends around uniquely delicious food.

My hopes for you with this cookbook are these three things:

- May you open your mind to new and exciting flavors cooked over the flames.

- May you feel empowered to try novel ideas and explore nontraditional dishes.

- May you experience that moment of joy, surrounded by fire, food, and friends, that you live to recreate just like it's the first time.

—Derek Wolf

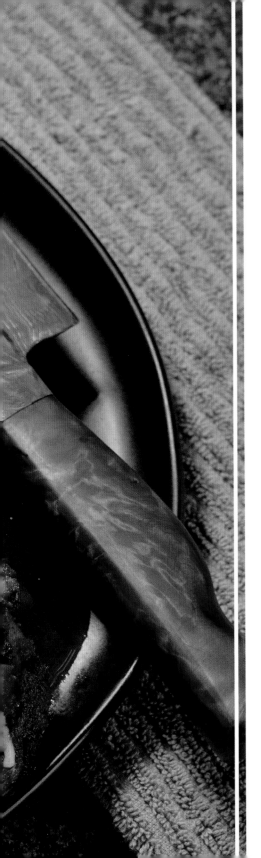

1
TASTE, FLAVOR, AND FIRE

I absolutely love food. But food is more than just food, right? Food is comfort to the soul, a vehicle to express yourself, and a demonstration of love to those you cook for. Although I explored the concept of fire cooking techniques, grilling, and more in my first book, *Food by Fire*, this book dives deeper into the passion I have for exploring the flavors of food created by fire. How does food get its unique flavor? How can I enhance a food's flavor over the fire? What do flavor and taste really mean, anyway? These are just a few questions that started my journey to *Flavor by Fire*.

Although this chapter will cover both taste and flavor, it's important to note that many books do this, too—and go deeper. What makes my approach, and thus this book, unique is that combination of cooking with fire to purposefully create all new flavor profiles on food. The heat and smoke produced by fire change the color, texture, and taste of just about every food there is, which for me, always comes back to the meat. Every type of protein has its own inherent flavor, which combines optimally with specific flavors and cooks uniquely over the flames. It takes a lot of practice to learn how to maximize the flavor of each protein. I do this every day and, in this book, share my experience with you in the hopes you can go further, faster with this knowledge.

Put this all together and you have a blueprint for the foundation we will establish in this chapter: learning about taste and flavor, then exploring the interaction of the specific food with fire to create flavor. In the chapters that follow, we'll connect the concepts using some of my favorite meats and recipes. To start, use this book as a guide, but once you master the fundamentals, get ready to explore new flavors on your own!

TASTE

Taste . . . and flavor . . . though we use these terms interchangeably, they do not actually mean the same thing. And, so, before diving into flavor, I want to first explore taste. I am not a food scientist, so I'm not going to go off the deep end here, but what I think is most important to understand is, taste is *only* the perception of a substance created by the taste buds on your tongue. Those perceptions, generally, can be grouped into five different categories: salty, sour, bitter, sweet, and umami. That means, when it comes to food, taste is a big piece, but still only a piece, of the flavor we experience when we eat. It's the umami of a luscious prime rib or the sour hit of a juicy lime.

Research has shown that taste served an evolutionary purpose for humans, helping us identify foods that could harm, such as poisonous plants or spoiled meat, versus nourish. Today, though, we tend to think about taste more with regard to enjoyment, not survival. Taste is also tied to cultural preferences in different ways. You might notice recipes from certain cultures or geographies are more sour than others, like American recipes, which are more reliant on sugar (sweet). And regardless of culture, personal preferences vary wildly regarding taste. For example, I prefer more salt on my food than my wife does. You can probably think of a few examples off the top of your head as well: You may like the bitterness of an IPA more than some of your friends, or someone in your family may be known as the one with a sweet tooth.

This variation from person to person poses an issue for recipe writers—like me! When I write a recipe, I have to be aware of the amount of salt used and make sure the final taste will please people like me as well as people like my wife. The same is true for sweet, bitter, and sour. All these tastes can become overpowering or present as underwhelming. Taste is a powerful influencer, and once you have a firm understanding of taste in general and your taste preferences, you will understand the first building block to making great food.

Hanging Leg of Lamb with Chimichurri Aioli, page 191

The Five Major Categories of Taste

Here, we'll discover what makes each taste unique, how to recognize it, and the reasons we are able to notice them all together. Let's dive in.

Salty

In my opinion, salt is the best place to begin when it comes to taste. Salt is part of most meals and the foundation of taste. It is also essential to our body's proper function. Sodium is something we need every day, and our ability to detect the taste of salt easily is believed to help us regulate our sodium intake. Salt can be made by combining sodium and chloride along with other minerals—classic table salt. However, salt can also be gathered and dried from seawater (sea salt) and from mineral deposits (pink Himalayan salt).

- **Types of salt used in this book**: Kosher salt (I like Morton brand), sea salt (coarse and fine)

Sour

Tart and powerful, sour is a taste some enjoy more than others. It is believed that the ability to taste sour could help humans detect toxic or spoiled foods (think of milk that's gone bad) as well as helping detect ripeness. Acid and sour go together, as foods with high acid content tend to have a sour taste on the palate. A classic example is citric acid, found in limes, lemons, and other citrus fruits. When used in cooking, citrus can brighten a dish with a slight tart taste. You can also experience this with vinegar (acetic acid) in combination with fatty foods, which might look like adding a vinegar-y chimichurri to a fatty picanha to help "cut" the fat and create a well-balanced dish (something we will discuss more on page 78).

- **Types of vinegar and citrus used in this book:** apple cider vinegar, lemon juice, lime juice, and red wine vinegar, white vinegar

Grilled Lamb Chops with Ancho Lemon Vinaigrette, page 188
Pickled Red Onions, page 54

Fruit is essential to adding that burst of sour and sweet to your food. Not only does fruit create fresh flavor, but it can also help tenderize your protein for the grill. Here is a quick breakdown of my favorite fruits and how to cook with them:

Cherry

FLAVOR: Tart, powerful with a hint of sweetness

COOKING METHODS: Using cherries when cooking is a little different from other fruits because of how powerfully flavorful they are. I prefer to use them most often in glazes for duck, in chutneys, and with chipotles in barbecue sauces.

Grapefruit

FLAVOR: Tart with a slightly sweet and bitter finish

COOKING METHODS: This is a great citrus fruit for winter grilling or adding a hint of bitterness to a dish. Grapefruit is delicious and fresh. With its inherent tartness, try grapefruit in a salmon glaze or pork ribs barbecue, or on any holiday dish to brighten it.

Lemon

FLAVOR: Bright, fresh, moderately sour with some sweetness

COOKING METHODS: Use lemon in just about any dish, especially for brined pork chops, marinated leg of lamb, or simply charred over the fire as a garnish (when grilled, lemons become sweeter). Lemon is an all-purpose citrus fruit that works well over fire.

Lime

FLAVOR: Sour, fresh with a slight hint of sweetness

COOKING METHODS: Limes have a sourness that can pair well with saltier, more savory foods. Try lime in marinades with tougher cuts, like skirt steak, or in a quick marinade for shrimp. Limes also goes well in sauces like charred salsas, flavored butters, and gremolata.

Orange

FLAVOR: Fresh and very sweet

COOKING METHODS: Oranges can make any dish stand out. Add orange juice to a carne asada marinade or a maple glaze for salmon. This sweet and powerful citrus fruit can be used in summer or winter to enhance any food.

Pineapple

FLAVOR: Bright, sweet, and slightly tart

COOKING METHODS: Pineapple is an amazing meat tenderizer because of its inherent capability to break down protein. Try pineapple in your marinade for huli huli chicken, in teriyaki glazes, or as a natural sweetener in a barbecue sauce. Just be careful when marinating with pineapple, as it can cause some proteins to over marinate and become mushy.

Bitter

Bitter is a taste that most Western cultures are not fond of consuming—or, at the very least, need to warm up to. This might be because the perception of bitter is believed to have developed to help humans detect toxins and poison. Although we commonly consume foods with some bitterness, including beer, coffee, grapefruit, and some vegetables, there are a couple of interesting things to note. People are more likely to dislike grapefruit than sweeter citrus fruits like oranges. Bitter is often paired with sweet. That taste combination might be natural, like with beer and grapefruit, or added by the consumer, as many people do when they put sugar in their coffee. When you're cooking, keep in mind that bitter is a great palate cleanser as well as a good masking agent. For example, Brad Prose taught me this trick: If you spritz coffee (bitter) onto wild game while cooking it, the coffee will help minimize the "gaminess." Bitter ingredients can also be used in marinades to complement sweet or sour tastes. In short, bitter is a great equalizer and really helps bring dishes into balance.

- **Types of bitter tastes used in this book:** arugula, beer, coffee, grapefruit, kale

Sweet

Moving in the opposite direction of bitter, it's safe to say we all love the taste of sweet. It can make just about anything better (including a bad day!). Found in sugar, the taste of sweetness is believed to help regulate carbohydrates in our body. Carbs are an essential component of our body's functioning, so making sure we get enough can be vital. You can easily get your sweet fix with foods such as honey, maple syrup, and a variety of fruits. Sweetness can help smooth out sharp tastes, like saltiness. Just think about a sweet glaze on a pork chop or dipping salty French fries into a milkshake.

- **Types of sweets used in this book:** agave nectar, brown sugar, honey, maple syrup

Umami/Savory

Last on the list, and last to be discovered, is umami, or savory, taste. Derived from the Japanese word meaning "delicious taste," I describe umami as meaty, hearty, and filling. This taste is believed to help us regulate the amount of protein we consume, and is a taste classically found in fish sauce, most meats, soy sauce, and more. Umami/savory taste is my absolute favorite of the five (for obvious reasons)—it makes a good dish great when used properly. Adding soy sauce to a marinade can elevate the other tastes to another level. You'll find this is true, too, with broths, cheeses, mushrooms, and steaks—their umami tastes elevate foods to that next umami level. Umami makes everything better, period.

- **Types of umami tastes in this book**: cheese, fish, fish sauce, meat, soy sauce

A Word on Spiciness

I believe that the heat level, or spiciness, of a food is a key element of flavor but *not* a taste. Although including jalapeños, hot sauce, and other spicy ingredients in dishes can add lots of different tastes to the food, spiciness is about the sensation perceived by the pain receptors in your mouth, not your taste buds. You are more than welcome to disagree with me!

Balancing and Boosting Taste

Although I have been focusing on single tastes so far, it's important to keep in mind that every food is not just one singular taste—except salt, if you taste it on its own. There is a complexity in the food we eat, and knowing that something can be more than just one taste is the next step to understanding taste's contribution to flavor.

All foods can carry many different tastes at the same time, even foods as "simple" as grilled steak. Though savory by nature, steak can also be salty because of seasoning, and bitter from the char it picks up while cooking. There may also be sweet or sour notes present, depending on the marinade or seasonings used. Although you can keep going, in this book, I focus on the primary taste of a dish along with a secondary taste to boost or balance that primary taste and provide more complex flavor.

Boosting and balancing occur when you add a complementary taste to a dish, whether by seasoning, cooking style, or finishing sauce, to accentuate, add nuance, or provide a counterpoint to a powerful taste inherent in the food. When you *boost* taste, you *highlight* the primary taste in the dish to make it more powerful. When you *balance* taste, you *equalize* a powerful taste to bring the overall taste into harmony.

Take that grilled steak—you could add a sour sauce, like chimichurri, to boost the steak's salty taste. You could also season the steak with a coffee-based rub or cook it in the coals to add a slight bitter finish. In the recipes that follow, I highlight a primary taste along with its boost or balance. This will help you quickly grasp the basic taste components of each dish. Here is a quick breakdown of classic boosting and balancing combinations between the major tastes:

Taste	Boost	Balance
SALTY	Sour, Sweet, Umami/Savory	Bitter
SOUR	Salty, Umami/Savory	Bitter, Sweet
BITTER	None	Salty, Sweet, Umami/Savory
SWEET	Salty, Umami/Savory	Bitter, Sour
UMAMI/SAVORY	Salty, Sour, Sweet	Bitter

FLAVOR

Compared to taste, flavor is a less defined concept and more of a moment when you interact with food. Some people say "flavor" is just the combination of taste and aroma; but for most people, including me, there is more to flavor than that.

Think about flavor this way (and feel free to pick a recipe from your childhood). I believe nobody can make my mother's macaroni and cheese recipe with the same flavor it has when I enjoy it at her house. I've found that no matter how hard I try to replicate her recipe, she always makes it just a little bit better. Hers is better, not because the ingredients are different or some

secret cooking technique she uses, but because the *flavor* is not totally replicable. Yes, she's spent years perfecting that outside crust and finding the ideal serving temperature. But there's also the nostalgia of being in her home, with the slight aroma of lavender in the kitchen. The experience of sitting down with my parents, of seeing it served from the same casserole dish she used while I was growing up . . . it all combines to make a difference in the perceived flavor.

Breaking Down Flavor

When you combine the sensation delivered by your taste buds with all the sensory details of the dish itself, you have a better understanding of overall flavor. Yet, unlike taste, there is a lack of consensus regarding what should be considered when thinking about the flavor of a dish. When I evaluate what I think goes into flavor, I arrive at the key components being: taste (see page 14), aroma, temperature, texture, experience and fire (see page26).

Aroma

With most food, its aroma registers well before we take that first bite because the smell of the food cooking hits our noses so quickly. (This is doubly true while grilling or barbecuing, as you'll smell the meat while it's cooking!)

Keep in mind that although many smells are closely linked in the brain to taste, all aromas are not created equally. Take, for example, some sour-related aromas. On one hand, if you can smell fresh lime in the air while cooking carne asada or chile-lime shrimp, your mouth will probably start to water. That bright citrus aroma is attractive and enticing. On the other hand, if you're spritzing vinegar on meat while barbecuing, the sharpness of the aroma can be a little off-putting. The results will be delicious, but smelling fresh vinegar just does not bring to mind the same fresh taste as fresh lime.

What's more, any aroma can be pleasing in a small amount, or off-putting when taken too far. Look no further than cooking a steak over fire as the perfect example. A well-caramelized steak will have a slightly sweet, smoky aroma as it cooks. But if you take it too far and burn the meat, the smoky aroma becomes acrid and no longer appetizing.

Aroma can make or break a dish's flavor. Having powerful yet attractive aromas to bring hungry people to the table is essential for having enjoyable food.

Grilled Chicken Breast with Spicy Mango Salsa, page 128

Temperature/Heat

When it comes to a food's temperature, you could identify a couple of things. There is the physical temperature of the food; being served hot, cold, or room temperature; and how it affects flavor. A classic example is pizza: delicious hot, with melting cheese and sizzling toppings, it can also be delicious leftover and cold, straight from the fridge. For most recipes in this book, the food is served warm or hot, right off the fire or out of the skillet. But, if you have leftovers, try the same dish cold and see how temperature affects flavor. It can be a dramatic difference.

What about the other form of heat? Although spice level might not be a taste, it can certainly affect flavor in a big way. Adding heat to your recipes can elevate savory character or saltiness in a dish without adding more salt. Spice can be added in many ways—from a black pepper crust on a brisket to a hit of cayenne in a pork rub. Keep in mind, though, many times heat and spice are a package deal with another taste: for example, pepper sauces often have some form of vinegar in them, to add a bright, tangy sourness to a dish along with spice. In this book, using spice wisely to enrich taste and flavor is always my goal.

Texture

Texture is something we experience alongside taste. There's no arguing that the feel and consistency of something in your mouth can change how much you enjoy it, or not—look no further than an overcooked steak, whose chewy, tough texture can ruin even the most expertly seasoned, high-quality cut. The texture of food can have many different expressions: crispy, fatty, oily, soft, tough, and more. And though there is no universally preferred texture for everyone, going back to that steak, I prefer a thick, crispy crust on my steak, whereas some people prefer the entire steak to have a buttery smooth texture. Going even further, even the cut of steak that people prefer relates to texture. Some enjoy a sirloin steak, which is tougher with more of a bite, whereas others will only order filet mignon because of how tender it is.

Texture can be a fun way to make a dish more interesting. Topping a grilled steak with crispy onions can create a more well-rounded texture. Serving a creamy sauce with a grilled salmon can make for a pleasing textural combination. Creating texture can be achieved by adding something to a dish, or by creation through the cooking process—either way, it can elevate your food and make it more enjoyable.

Experience

The final element of flavor is the experience itself. Although this might sound esoteric, it is something that affects everyone. Experience around food can mean everything from the people you are enjoying it with, the place where you are eating, the occasion, atmosphere, or the moment you discover a new favorite food.

As I said earlier, I will never forget the first time I cooked over a fire: skirt steak and chimichurri. Eating that meal with my wife will live in my memory forever because it was the meal that started this whole journey for us. To this day, every time my wife and I see skirt steak and chimichurri on a menu, we have to try it—not out of pride for our cooking, but because when we eat that meal, it transports us to a simpler time. (A time when I did not always smell like fire and smoke. A time when we did not have thirty-plus grills in our backyard or two freezers full of meat. A time when something so simple, like steak and chimichurri, was revolutionary to our palate.) In any case, that example is extreme but shows how the experience we have with food often ties our past to our present, and can even make us excited for the future. And, although it might be the last piece of the flavor puzzle, experience around food brings everything else into harmony.

Going further, experience is part of the reason so many amazing chefs are not afraid to share their recipes. Even if you make their dish at home and it turns out delicious, it will never perfectly replicate the flavor of the same dish when eaten at their restaurant. As many of us have figured out: there's more to a dish than just ingredients and cooking technique.

Food is an expression of yourself and often of the love you have for others. The same thing goes for flavor. If food is the noun; flavor is the verb. If food is love, then flavor is the warm hug. Flavor is the experience of that love and affection found not just in the food but also in the people who make it and enjoy it with you.

FIRE

You might be wondering how fire fits into this world of taste and flavor? Although there are many ways fire can contribute to the flavor, I believe the two most important components of fire are *heat* and *smoke*; each component brings a unique characteristic to the food while transforming its overall flavor profile.

Heat

When I speak of grilling or cooking directly over the fire, I am talking about cooking with flames or hot coals. This cooking process is perfect for any quick-and-easy cooking, especially for thinner cuts of meat or vegetables. How grilling or cooking over fire affects the food's flavor, though, is through a complex chemical process called the Maillard reaction. To oversimplify, the Maillard reaction is the transformation of proteins and sugars through the use of heat on the food to create browning and whole new flavors. This reaction occurs at its full strength above 300°F (150°C), causing fast color and flavor changes to the food, which is why most grilling and direct cooking recipes call for temperatures in this range, or higher. This is a distinctive feature that sets grilling apart from other cooking methods!

Let's look at this reaction as it occurs with a simple grilled steak. When cooked over a high-heat fire, the steak will begin to change from a ruby-red color to a deep, dark brown developing a thick crust and a distinctive savory, sweet, and bitter taste and aroma. This is what we hope for when we grill meat over open flames. We love that deep sear on the outside of the meat that opens to reveal a beautiful tender center. The flavor of grilled meat is also powerful and attractive. The charred edges give us a nice bitterness that helps amplify the savoriness of the steak. And the crust has a slight hint of sweetness from the browning of the sugars.

This is the reason seared or grilled meat will always be better than, say, a dull, gray boiled steak. The crust, flavor, and taste of the fire make it crave-able. The smoky aroma is something that intoxicates us and keeps us coming back for more. However, direct fire cooking is only the tip of the iceberg for smoky flavor.

Ancho Coffee Hanging Tomahawks with Blue Cheese Sauce, page 57

Smoke

When it comes to cooking indirectly over the fire, you unlock different flavor profiles compared to direct cooking. The keys to cooking indirectly have to do not only with the Maillard reaction, but intramuscular fat and additional smoky flavor. Yes, we are back with the Maillard reaction but this time it is gentler, with temperatures under 300°F (150°C). And, although when direct cooking over the fire you see quick changes to the meat, the process of cooking indirectly takes a longer time to develop similar flavors. Why spend the extra time? Because there are other advantages to cooking this way! When using cuts of meat with high amounts of intermuscular fat—for example cuts such as brisket, pork butt, and pork ribs—the only way to let that fat melt and extract all of the meat's savory, delicious flavor is by cooking it low and slow over indirect heat. Most cuts used for this style of cooking would not be very tender if cooked over high heat in a shorter time, and would likely become burnt! Therefore, by smoking this meat, we develop a similar outside crust (called bark), melt the intermuscular fat, and create a very juicy, tender meal.

That said, with shorter cooking times you can achieve delicious results smoking delicate fish, shrimp, lean cuts of protein, or even steak because you can control the temperature more easily than over higher heat. Shrimp and fish can be cooked with more accuracy when they are smoked.

Note: I also love reverse searing! If you're not familiar with the process, reverse searing is done by first smoking a cut of meat at a low temperature, to your desired internal temperature, resting it, and then searing the meat over high heat to develop that beautiful crust. This cooking method ensures that leaner cuts (or steaks) are cooked accurately and to your preferred temperature without the fear of overcooking the meat using high heat exclusively.

Keep the Smoke Blue

As anyone who has tasted barbecue knows, smoke changes the flavor of meat. When cooking low and slow with live coals or fire, you will appreciate this very pleasant smoky flavor . . . if you manage the fire and smoke correctly. The smoke should always be blue and nearly clear while cooking—never cook with that thick, white smoke that develops as you get a fire or smoker started. White smoke will deposit an unpleasant layer of impurities on the outside of the food, giving it a powerful and overwhelming smoke flavor. Blue smoke is cleaner and mild. Remember, you want tender, flavorful, delicious barbecue, not meat you can't taste because the smoke is so strong!

FIRE COOKING BASICS

In my first cookbook, *Food by Fire*, I dove deep into some of my favorite cooking methods and processes. In this book, I am not going to cover all the same topics in depth here, but I will provide all the essentials you need to cook the recipes in this book! This section should get you fully equipped to cook over fire, even if it's your first time giving it a try.

Essential Gear

My kitchen is filled to the brim with cooking gear. Even if yours is not, I assume you'll have a few basic tools, like good quality tongs, knives, and cutting boards. Here is my list of essentials that may already be part of your kitchen or that you may want to add to your arsenal:

Cast-iron skillet: A good quality cast-iron skillet is indispensable when cooking both delicate and heartier foods over the flames. It heats evenly and retains the heat for an even cook.

Grill: I have both expensive and cheap grills, and almost any grill will serve for cooking these recipes! Most grills can easily cook directly, but if you plan to cook indirect as well, make sure you have a decent lid or grill cover.

Heat-resistant gloves: Don't burn yourself! I recommend welding gloves.

Meat thermometer: This tool offers peace of mind to know when your food is cooked to the right, and safe, temperature for maximum flavor and food safety.

Types of Fires

Direct Fire (One-Zone Fire)

Direct fire cooking is your classic grilling style with one heat source and no cooler areas on the grill. It is ideal for high-heat cooking, cooking with a cast-iron skillet, and more. Direct fire cooking creates delicious grilled food very quickly and can be fueled with hardwood or lump charcoal. My only tip is, if you can afford it, a grill grate that can raise and lower food relative to the heat will increase your satisfaction with this cooking style. Although you'll still be locked in to the high heat below the food, having the ability to cool the temperature by raising the grill away from the heat opens up a world of possibilities.

Two-Zone Fire

This cooking style is the traditional *indirect* cooking method. To set up a two-zone fire, split your grilling space in half, with one side holding the heat (wood or coals) and the other side empty. The idea is to be able to utilize the high heat when needed, then push the meat to the cool side if you need to slow the cooking process. A two-zone fire can be used for low and slow cooking, keeping the meat only on the cool side of the grill and cooking it for a long time. As you get comfortable with this setup, I encourage you to try searing the meat over high heat to develop a crust, then pulling it over to finish cooking on the cool side. This gives more control over the sear and results in juicier meat.

Note: Make sure the cool side of your grill is on the side with your grill's chimney. This helps create a nice airflow that maintains even heat and creates a better smoke flavor.

Three-Zone Fire

Last, there's the three-zone fire. This cooking method splits your grilling surface into three even segments, with the fire on the outside ends and a cool spot in the middle. A three-zone fire is excellent for cooking very fatty cuts of meat on skewers and for setting up a rotisserie. Having that cool center gives you a spot to place a drip pan under to catch fat drippings that would otherwise cause flare-ups. This setup helps create a more even heat for cooking the food and prevents burning it. If using a skewer or rotisserie, this setup also makes it easier to achieve an even crust on the food while helping to speed along the cooking process. You can use this method in an open fire pit or with an enclosed grill.

Starting a Fire with Wood

Learning to start a fire properly can make a huge difference in your cooks. Although there are many ways to start a fire, I prefer the "log cabin method." Basically, you build a square stacked fire with thinner cuts of wood in the middle, which will create an even heat for the cook and a long-lasting fire.

1. Begin by splitting logs into 10 to 12 pieces. Aim for a range of widths in your pieces, with the most important pieces being the thin shavings.

2. Lay 2 medium-size pieces of wood parallel to each, 2 to 3 inches (5 to 7.5 cm) apart. Place natural fire starters in the middle of the two logs and light the starters.

3. Build another layer on top with 2 similar-size pieces of wood, perpendicular to the logs below them. Between the second layer of logs, add 1 or 2 thin slices of wood that will catch fire very easily.

4. Continue building layers, repeating step 3, until you have 4 to 6 layers total. Let the fire burn naturally for 30 to 40 minutes.

5. Once the wood pieces begin to split in half from being burnt, push the pile close together. Start to check the fire for your desired cooking temperature.

6. When your fire is within the temperature for your cook, add your grill grate to preheat for 2 to 3 minutes.

7. Begin cooking! Add more wood or lump charcoal, as needed, to maintain the temperature.

Starting a Fire with Lump Charcoal

Another fuel source I enjoy using is lump charcoal, which creates a very even and clean heat without lots of ash or soot. Although both lump charcoal and briquettes are great fuel sources, I prefer lump charcoal because it generally provides a better flavor and is conducive to achieving higher temperatures. I also recommend getting a charcoal chimney (they are typically inexpensive)! Although you could try creating a fire with a mound of charcoal in your grill, a chimney makes starting that fire much easier.

1. Fill a charcoal chimney with lump charcoal. The amount of heat you need and the duration of the cook will determine how full you fill your chimney.

   - A full chimney will give off high levels of heat for 3 to 4 hours.

   - Two full chimneys will give off high levels of heat for 4 to 6 hours.

   - A half-full chimney will give off high heat for 1 to 2 hours.

2. Place your chimney on a fire-resistant surface or inside your unlit grill.

3. Arrange some newspaper (black-and-white pages only) or natural fire starters underneath the chimney and light them.

4. Let the chimney burn until most of the coals at the top of the chimney are glowing red hot.

5. When you are ready to use the charcoal, put on your gloves. Carefully lift the chimney by the handle and dump the coals into your grill or onto the fire, as needed.

BREAKDOWN OF FIRE TEMPERATURES

Low: 200°F to 250°F (93°C to 120°C)

Medium-Low: 250°F to 300°F (120°C to 150°C)

Medium: 300°F to 350°F (150°C to 180°C)

Medium-High:
350°F to 400°F (180°C to 200°C)

High: 400°F+ (200°C+)

INTERNAL TEMPERATURES FOR FOODS (AFTER RESTING)

BEEF:

   Blue: 100°F to 110°F (38°C to 43°C)

   Rare: 110°F to 120°F (43°C to 49°C)

   Medium-Rare:
120°F to 130°F (49°C to 54°C)

   Medium: 130°F to 140°F (54°C to 60°C)

   Well-Done: 140°F + (60°C+)

CHICKEN: 165°F (74°C) minimum

FISH AND SEAFOOD: 145°F (63°C)

GROUND MEAT: 160°F (71°C) minimum

PORK: 145°F (63°C) minimum; however, some cuts, such as pork shoulder or ribs, should reach the 200°F+ (93°C+) range to break down more of their fat.

RUBS AND SAUCES

Before we hit the recipes, let's discuss seasonings and sauces, the cornerstone for well-flavored food that can make or break a dish. The challenge is, there are so many seasonings and spices available, it can be overwhelming to know where to start! Trust me, I understand the feeling. That is why I have included these fantastic seasonings and sauces to get you started.

I have created many seasoning blends over my time cooking, but I always come back to simple, all-purpose (AP) seasonings. These AP seasonings enhance just about anything! I start with two all-purpose blends—OTFC All-Purpose BBQ Seasoning, page 38, and OTFC All-Purpose Beef Rub, page 39—that focus on barbecue and steak. Both are versatile for cooking, give great flavor, and set a foundation for the dish. The third seasoning, my Ancho Coffee Rub (page 40), is very useful, as it contributes both sweet and bitter flavors to food.

Next, you'll find my go-to barbecue sauces: OTFC Spicy BBQ Sauce (page 41) and OTFC Sweet BBQ Sauce (page 43). These are similar sauces, but divulge with their own crazy fun flavors once you start to cook them. I love making these sauces in large batches to keep in mason jars in the fridge, as they are used as part of many dishes throughout the book. Feel free to experiment with the sauces to make them your own. Although these are my favorite variations, there is so much more you could add. Make them spicier with habanero or sweeter with molasses. Tweak them to your liking on your quest to discover new flavors.

OTFC ALL-PURPOSE BBQ SEASONING

Making barbecue seasoning is an art form. There are so many ways you can approach seasoning that it can be daunting just to start! My partnership with Spiceology to create spice blends helped me navigate the process of making good seasonings. This all-purpose seasoning is one I continually reach for when making something simple and easy on my 'que. There are a few special ingredients required (that can easily be found on Spiceology.com), but that can also be substituted. If you don't have maple sugar, try simple cane sugar! As for the orange peel powder, zest your own oranges to get the same flavor. This makes an insanely versatile rub for pork butts, ribs, steaks, and more.

PREP TIME: 5 MINUTES

Yield: Makes 4 ounces (115 g), enough to season 3 or 4 racks of ribs or 2 pork shoulders

2 tablespoons (30 g) brown sugar

1 tablespoon (15 g) kosher salt

1 tablespoon (8.4 g) smoked paprika

2½ teaspoons granulated garlic

1½ teaspoons onion powder

1½ teaspoons maple sugar

1 teaspoon orange peel powder

½ teaspoon red pepper flakes

SPECIAL GEAR

None

In a small bowl, stir together all the ingredients. Use about 1 tablespoon (19 g) per 1½ pounds (681 g) of meat to season any meat you smoke or barbecue. Store any unused seasoning in an airtight container, in a cool dry place, for 1 to 2 months.

OTFC ALL-PURPOSE BEEF RUB

Finding the right seasoning for beef can be hard—honestly, it's really hard to beat just salt, pepper, and garlic (SPG). So, you need a seasoning that will really bring the power to choose it over the classic SPG. This all-purpose beef rub is just that. Now, it does include salt, pepper, and garlic as its base, but it also holds some secrets that will make the flavor of every cut of steak pop from the grill. Beginning with chipotle flakes for smokiness and spiciness, which amp up the overall flavor. Next, onion, mustard, and cinnamon bring a subtle but not overpowering sweetness. Lastly, mesquite powder captures that full smoky savoriness I love on steak. If you do not have mesquite powder, replace the kosher salt with the same amount of smoked salt to add a nice hint of smokiness. This beef rub is perfect for just about any cut but tastes amazing on brisket, chuck roast, rib eyes, sirloin, and tri-tip.

PREP TIME: 5 MINUTES

Yield: Makes 3 ounces (85 g), enough to season 6 to 9 pounds (2.7 to 4 kg) of meat

2 tablespoons (30 g) kosher salt

1 tablespoon (8.5 g) black peppercorns, freshly cracked

1 tablespoon (10 g) dried minced garlic

2 teaspoons dried chipotle flakes

1½ teaspoons dried minced onion

1 teaspoon ground mustard

1 teaspoon ground cinnamon

½ teaspoon mesquite powder

SPECIAL GEAR

None

In a small bowl, stir together all the ingredients. Use about 1 tablespoon (14 g) per 1½ pounds (681 g) of meat to season any cut of beef you smoke or barbecue. Store any unused seasoning in an airtight container, in a cool dry place, for 1 to 2 months.

ANCHO COFFEE RUB

This is one of my favorite rubs for grilling and smoking. Coffee is something that a lot of people do not associate with rubs and seasoning. If you're one of those people, this rub will change your mind! Paired with ancho chile powder, this is a savory, slightly bitter, slightly sweet seasoning that pairs well with anything fatty. It's ideal for beef and pork cuts like brisket, pork shoulder, rib eye, skirt steak, or even pork belly. The coffee acts as both sweet and bitter tastes that mellow that heavy fattiness. Serve the rub with some grilled steak and eggs for breakfast or add it to a marinade, where its unique flavor will shine.

PREP TIME: 5 MINUTES

Yield: Makes 3 ounces (85 g), enough to season 6 to 9 pounds (2.7 to 4 kg) of meat

1½ tablespoons (7.5 g) medium-grind coffee (preferably dark roast)

2 tablespoons (30 g) kosher salt

1 tablespoon (7.5 g) ancho chile powder

2 teaspoons garlic powder

1½ teaspoons brown sugar

1½ teaspoons onion powder

1½ teaspoons ground cumin

1½ teaspoons freshly ground black pepper

1 teaspoon ground cinnamon

SPECIAL GEAR

None

In a small bowl, stir together all the ingredients. Use about 1 tablespoon (11 g) per 1½ pounds (681 g) of meat to season any type of meat you smoke or barbecue. Store any unused seasoning in an airtight container, in a cool dry place, for 1 to 2 months.

OTFC SPICY BBQ SAUCE

Everyone needs a good, spicy barbecue sauce ready to be used at any moment. This sauce is perfect for just about anything cooked in a pit. The heat comes from the cayenne pepper and cayenne-based hot sauce. If you prefer a tabasco-based hot sauce, use that instead! There's a slight hint of smokiness from the chipotle puree that adds savory notes to the heat. You can find chipotle puree at most grocery stores or Latin American groceries. If you can't find it, puree two or three chipotles in adobo sauce (about 2 tablespoons (14g) total) instead. Make sure to keep the sauce over an even medium-low heat, at a nice simmer, and leave it uncovered to thicken. Serve with chicken lollipops (see page 121), ribs, or drizzle over twice-baked potatoes cooked over the fire.

PREP TIME: 10 MINUTES | COOK TIME: 40 MINUTES

Yield: Makes 2 cups (about 400 g)

1 cup (240 g) ketchup

2 tablespoons (25 g) sugar

2½ tablespoons (17.5 g) chipotle puree

2 tablespoons (30 m) white vinegar

1½ tablespoons (23 ml) cayenne-based hot sauce

1½ tablespoons (30 g) honey

1 tablespoon (9 g) garlic powder

1½ teaspoons onion powder

1½ teaspoons cayenne pepper

Kosher salt

Freshly ground black pepper

SPECIAL GEAR
None

In a skillet over medium-low heat, stir together all the ingredients, seasoning with salt and pepper to taste, and bring to a boil. Cook, uncovered, for 30 to 35 minutes, stirring occasionally, until the sauce is thickened to your liking. Refrigerate the sauce in an airtight container for up to 1 week.

OTFC SWEET BBQ SAUCE

When it comes to classic sweet barbecue sauces, this one is both easy and flavorful. With its sweet hint from brown sugar and honey, this sauce pairs well with chicken lollipops (see page 121), pulled pork, smoked ribs, and more. The key is keeping the sauce at a low simmer, with the lid off, so moisture can evaporate, until it thickens. If you like a sweeter sauce, add a little more brown sugar. If you prefer a little more tang, substitute white vinegar for the apple cider vinegar, which will add a nice sourness to the sauce to balance the sweetness. This tasty all-around barbecue sauce is built for anything you cook in the backyard.

PREP TIME: 10 MINUTES | COOK TIME: 40 MINUTES

Yield: Makes 2 cups
(about 500 g)

1 cup (240 g) ketchup

¼ cup (80 g) honey

2 tablespoons (30 g) brown
sugar

2 tablespoons (30 g)
stoneground mustard

2 tablespoons (30 ml) apple
cider vinegar

1 tablespoon (15 ml)
Worcestershire sauce

1 tablespoon (9 g) garlic
powder

1½ teaspoons onion powder

1 teaspoon hot sauce

Kosher salt

Freshly ground black pepper

SPECIAL GEAR

None

In a skillet over medium-low heat, stir together all the ingredients, seasoning with salt and pepper to taste, and bring to a boil. Cook, uncovered, for 30 to 35 minutes, stirring occasionally, until the sauce is thickened to your liking. Refrigerate the sauce in an airtight container for up to 1 week.

2
BEEF

This likely won't come as a surprise to those who have seen my recipes online: I love beef. Most cuts of beef are so easy to cook over fire that it feels like it was the original meat to touch the flames. Whether you are grilling a bone-in rib eye or smoking a whole brisket, beef is superb at absorbing smoke and fire flavor from the grill. You can create a beautiful crust when searing beef in cast iron and achieve amazing grill marks when you cook it on the grill.

Although it is easy to love beef, it can be overwhelming to choose from all those cuts offered at the butcher's counter. Over the past couple of years, there has been a resurgence of interest in butchery, which has led to the average home chef learning more about butcher cuts. What is a butcher cut? There are different definitions, but to me, a butcher cut is one of the non-prized, or leftover, cuts of meat that the butcher would often take—those steaks or roasts with a ton of fat, or cuts requiring special knowledge to cook, or, due to trends, something that just might not sell easily. Over the years, these cuts have included hanger steaks, picanha, skirt steaks, teres major, and more.

So, in addition to the common cuts of meat you usually think of cooking over the flame, it was important to me to cook nontraditional butcher cuts here, too, to fully explore the flavors of beef. Don't get me wrong: There are plenty of recipes that use common cuts here, but I also call for specific, lesser-known cuts to try to bring out flavors you might have never had before. Let's get grilling.

BEEF AND TASTE

As with most meats, beef has an inherent umami/savory taste. It is satisfying on the palate, pairs nicely with salt, and is complemented by sour tastes as well. (That is why I love skirt steak with chimichurri.) Prepared simply, beef is a classic crowd-pleaser. In this chapter, we will not only accentuate beef's natural umami qualities, but also boost and balance that umami with salty, sour, bitter, and sweet tastes. My goal here is to build flavor complexity without losing the essence of what makes beef great to begin with. Let's talk about how beef pairs with the five major flavors.

Salty

Salt is the classic taste to use with beef. Many people love using only coarse salt on their steaks to keep it natural without too many other tastes overpowering the meat's taste. Salt helps to develop great crusts on your grilled steaks, and lets the beef stand alone as the star of the dinner show. I think salt is a fantastic partner for beef used this way and a great ingredient for increasing beef's tenderness when it's used for dry brining.

Sour

This is one of my favorite tastes to use in marinades or as a sauce for beef. Because citric acid helps break down meat and make it more tender, using lemons, limes, or oranges in marinades provides both taste and texture improvements for tougher cuts of beef, like skirt or flank steak. Sour also pairs well with fatty cuts of beef, often balancing the heartiness of the meat without sacrificing flavor. For example, a vinegar-based sauce or a side of pickled vegetables can cut through fatty meats like brisket, making it even more enjoyable.

Bitter

A tricky taste to add to beef, bitter is a taste that can be coaxed out naturally through cooking. Think back to your last bite of a slightly charred piece of steak: It is slightly bitter. You can even capitalize on that bitterness with some fatty cuts: the richness and char can become the cornerstone of a dish. You can even increase the bitter factor by cooking the steaks right in the coals, which provides a charcoal-like bitter flavor that just tastes right on steak.

Sweet

To be honest, sweet and beef are not the easiest pairing. It's easy to accidentally go too far and end up with a dish that is super sweet (which is not something I enjoy) or be underwhelmed with a sweetness that's barely noticeable—and what's the point of that? Through trial and error, I've found that using mild (less hoppy) beers or sweet condiments such as mirin and agave gives you that perfect sweet note without making your steak taste like sugar. You can also experiment with adding small amounts of sugar to your seasonings to achieve increased browning (which is flavor). Sugar can be the secret to a perfect crust without overcooking your beef.

Umami/Savory

As mentioned already, beef is inherently savory and it pairs well with additional savory flavors! For example, adding a little soy sauce to your marinades can create a lot more flavor depth in your dish. (It is one of my go-to ways to add savory to beef.) Another way you can turn up the intensity of savory is with bacon, butter, or bone marrow. All these ingredients can make any beef dish taste better (okay, maybe not *every* beef recipe, but you get the idea).

BEEF AND FLAVOR

When it comes to enjoying beef, aroma, temperature, texture, and experience are incredibly important—from the tantalizing aroma to the signature sizzle to the delicious memories of cooking favorite cuts over the fire—and other nuances you should pay attention to as well.

Aroma

Beef has such strong savoriness that it can permeate a whole house when cooking indoors. The aroma alone gets people running to the dinner table! That unique smell, which can also be your secret weapon, comes primarily from the fat (or tallow) of the beef. Use the fat to your advantage and baste your next steak with beef tallow to take it to another level! Add a little rosemary, thyme, and garlic and you are sure to have a steak with incredible aroma.

Temperature/Heat

Beef can stand up to spiciness quite well. I have found that dried chiles, such as ancho, chipotle, or New Mexico, nicely complement beef's savory qualities while still bringing a nice heat. Fresh chiles pair well with beef as part of marinades or sauces. I love using jalapeños in sauces like my Creamy Corn Salsa (page 50) as it can bring a complementary freshness to a charred steak. And, because chiles like jalapeño and habanero can be overpowering, using them to tenderize the meat lets the beef shine.

Texture

I would say that beef has a wide variety of textures when compared to other meats. And although most beef cuts are firmer than the average meat, there are some very tender, succulent cuts, such as tenderloin or teres major. Still, the firmness of a beef steak is what gives it that classic crave-able heartiness.

The key to understanding beef and texture is understanding how to use this heartiness to your advantage. Beef cuts such as rib eyes and strip steaks are soft and tender enough that you can focus on developing amazing crust and crispiness on the outside. The combination of salting at the right time, high heat from the fire, and the preparation of the skillet/grill are the keys to achieving that nice crust. On the other hand, some of beef's toughest cuts create the most deliciously tenders meals when cooked low and slow—such as beef ribs or brisket.

Experience

Beef has always been a dichotomy of casualness and celebration. Most people have fond memories of casual summer cookouts or steak nights. At my house while I was growing up, steak night was something we did almost every week. The smell of Dad's homemade seasoning searing on his kettle grill is something I hope to recreate one day with my children. However, you may also have memories of steak eaten on special occasions—it's a food that is worthy of celebration!

Whether at a steakhouse for a birthday or feeding family come in town for a graduation or wedding, beef has always been part of something that means excitement, joy, and coming together for me.

BEEF AND FIRE

When you cook directly over the flames, beef tends to take on a charred umami taste from the high heat. You get that classic crispy outside crust with a slight smokiness from the flames. The other thing that grilled beef offers is that sweet yet slightly bitter char. In my opinion, there is nothing wrong with some char on your steaks. This might be controversial, but I say get rid of those grill marks!—a beautiful crust is what you want. That said, the char on steak can be slightly bitter from the beef fat crisping up, and also sweet from the browning effect from the flames.

When it comes to cooking indirectly, you can add tons of umami smokiness to that steak. Cuts such as brisket and chuck take on delicious savoriness from the blue smoke kissing the meat. The cuts that usually get cooked with indirect heat are big, fatty, and take a long time to cook, mostly because of the intermuscular fat that needs to be rendered to prevent the meat from being tough and chewy. These cuts get tons of smoky goodness on the outside, developing a different type of crust called *bark*. The bark develops when that slowly rendering fat, smoke, and your seasonings become one. Because the fat renders more slowly during indirect cooking, the crust will not be as crunchy as what you can achieve with direct cooking, but it will pack a huge flavor punch.

The combination of all these tastes and flavors delivers a delicious dish made with beef. Now, let's cook some food!

BEER-MARINATED BAVETTE STEAK WITH CREAMY CORN SALSA

Beer makes a great marinade for beef, as it creates a unique dual taste and flavor profile because of the hops. Hops gives beer that bitter flavor that is refreshing on a warm summer day and is the reason "hoppy" beers, like an IPA, tend to be more bitter. On the other hand, the malt in the beer provides sweetness. That bitter and sweet combination is what we want for this beer-marinated bavette steak! Using a light, less hoppy beer, gives us the sweet of the beer malt with a small amount of bitter from the meat. The caramelization of the sugars in the beer will further sweeten the steak and make it out-of-this-world delicious. Add a sweet creamy corn salsa, and you'll be in heaven.

PREP TIME: 20 MINUTES | MARINATE TIME: 4 HOURS | COOK TIME: 15 MINUTES

Yield: 4 servings

FOR BEER MARINADE

1 (12-ounce, or 360 ml) bottle of beer (preferably pale ale)

¼ cup (60 ml) soy sauce

4 or 5 garlic cloves, minced

1 tablespoon (15 ml) hot sauce

2 teaspoons kosher salt

2 teaspoons freshly ground black pepper

½ red onion, thinly sliced

Juice of 2 limes

Juice of 1 blood orange

1½ tablespoons (23 ml) canola oil

FOR STEAK

1 whole bavette/flap steak

FOR CREAMY CORN SALSA

3 or 4 ears corn, shucked

3 or 4 garlic cloves, minced

2 tablespoons (30 g) sour cream

2½ tablespoons (25 g) diced red onion

2 tablespoons (2 g) chopped fresh cilantro

2 tablespoons (14 g) grated Cotija cheese

1 tablespoon (9 g) diced jalapeño pepper

2 teaspoons hot sauce

Juice of 2 limes

SPECIAL GEAR

None

1. **To make the marinade**: In a gallon-size zip-top bag or large food-safe bowl, combine all the marinade ingredients and mix thoroughly.

2. **To make the steak**: Carefully add the steak to the marinade, seal the bag, and massage to coat the steak. Refrigerate for at least 4 hours to marinate, ideally overnight.

3. Preheat the grill for direct cooking over high heat (400°F, or 200°C).

4. **To make the corn salsa**: Place the corn on the grill and cook for 7 to 8 minutes, turning, or until softened.

5. As the corn cooks, remove the steak from the marinade and discard the marinade. Place the steak on the hottest part of the grill and cook for about 4 minutes per side, or until the internal temperature of the steak reaches 125°F (52°C) for medium-rare. Pull the steak and corn off the grill and let the steak rest for 5 to 7 minutes.

6. **To finish the salsa**: Slice the corn kernels off the cob and place them in a medium bowl. Stir in the remaining salsa ingredients and mix thoroughly.

7. Once the steak has rested, slice it thinly against the grain and top with the corn salsa for serving.

CHIPOTLE PEPPERCORN SMOKED BRISKET

With the perfect level of salt from its simple seasoning blend, this brisket also brings a little heat thanks to the freshly cracked peppercorns and smoky chipotle powder. The hint of white vinegar and hot sauce bring the sour notes and enough acid to cut through the salty, fatty brisket for the most amazing flavor.

PREP TIME: 20 MINUTES | BRINE TIME: 4 HOURS | COOK TIME: 16 HOURS, PLUS 1 HOUR TO REST

Yield: 10 servings

FOR SEASONING

¼ cup (72 g) coarse sea salt

¼ cup (24 g) freshly cracked black peppercorns

2 tablespoons (18 g) garlic powder

1½ tablespoons (11.25 g) chipotle powder

FOR BRISKET

1 whole (11- to 12-pound, or 5 to 5.4 kg) packer brisket

FOR SPRITZ

1 (12-ounce, or 360 ml) bottle lager

2 tablespoons (30 ml) white vinegar

2 teaspoons hot sauce

SPECIAL GEAR

Spritz bottle, butcher paper

1. **To make the seasoning**: In a small bowl, stir together the salt, pepper, garlic powder, and chipotle powder.

2. **To make the brisket**: Keeping your brisket cold, trim off any excess fat, leaving about ¼-inch (0.6 cm)-thick fat cap (anymore is too much). Coat the brisket thoroughly with the seasoning. Refrigerate the brisket, uncovered, to brine and rest for 4 to 12 hours.

3. Preheat the smoker for indirect cooking over medium-low heat (250°F, or 120°C). Add some mesquite or hickory wood chunks or chips to the smoker for more smoke flavor.

4. **To make the spritz**: In a 16-ounce (480 ml) spray-top bottle, combine all the spritz ingredients. Cover and shake well.

5. **To cook the brisket**: Place the brisket on the smoker, fat-side down, and cook for 1 hour.

6. Spray the brisket with the spritz and cook for 7 to 8 hours more, spraying the meat every hour, until it reaches 165°F (74°C).

7. While the brisket smokes, lay out two 2-by-4-foot (60 by 120 cm) pieces of butcher paper that slightly overlap.

8. Place the smoked brisket at one end of the butcher paper. Pull the paper over the brisket and tuck it underneath. Fold in the sides and begin to roll the meat over the butcher paper until it is completely wrapped. Place the wrapped brisket back into the smoker, fat-side up. Cook for 7 to 8 hours more until the internal temperature reaches between 202°F and 203°F (94°C and 95°C). Pull the brisket off the smoker and let rest at room temperature for 1 hour.

9. Unwrap the brisket and discard the butcher paper. Slice the brisket through the middle and separate the point from the flat. Slice the flat against the grain at the same angle as when you cut it in half. Rotate the point 90 degrees and slice it against the grain to serve.

SWEET CHILE–BRAISED BEEF TACOS WITH PICKLED RED ONIONS

There are not many foods so delicious they can be served at high-end restaurants or as late-night snack food! I think these tacos could go either way: dress them up for a fancy night in or serve them rustic on paper plates. The pickled red onions give you a crispy, sour companion for the rich beef, and while the onions do their thing, you'll braise some short ribs with a sweet sauce made with a blend of chiles, garlic, and agave nectar. If you're cooking for a crowd, double this dish. It's a fantastic dinner for the whole family and you'll want leftovers!

PREP TIME: 45 MINUTES | PICKLING TIME: 2 HOURS | COOK TIME: 5 HOURS

Yield: 6 servings

FOR PICKLED RED ONIONS

2 cups (480 ml) water

1½ cups (360 ml) white vinegar

¼ cup (50 g) sugar

2 teaspoons fine sea salt

1 or 2 red onions, thinly sliced

FOR SEASONING PASTE

4 dried ancho chiles, stemmed and seeded

3 dried guajillo chiles, stemmed and seeded

3 dried chipotle chiles, stemmed and seeded

8 to 10 garlic cloves, peeled

2 cups (480 ml) water, plus ¼ cup

2 tablespoons (12 g) freshly ground black pepper

1½ tablespoons (4.5 g) Mexican oregano

1½ tablespoons (30 g) agave nectar

1 tablespoon (18 g) fine sea salt

2 teaspoons ground cinnamon

1½ teaspoons ground nutmeg

FOR BEEF

8 or 9 bone-in English short ribs

1½ tablespoons (23 g) kosher salt

1 tablespoon (6 g) freshly ground black pepper

1 tablespoon (9 g) garlic powder

4 cups (960 ml) beef bone broth

1 (12-ounce, or 360 ml) bottle dark Mexican beer

2 bay leaves

FOR TACOS

8 to 10 flour or corn tortillas

Sour cream for garnish

Grated Cotija cheese for garnish

Chopped fresh cilantro for garnish

SPECIAL GEAR

Dutch oven, tripod

1. **To make the pickled red onions**: In a medium saucepan over medium-high heat, combine the water, vinegar, sugar, and salt. Simmer until the sugar and salt dissolve. Remove the pan from the heat and let the liquid cool. Place the onions into a 16-ounce (480 ml) mason jar and pour the cooled liquid over them until they're covered. Seal the jar and refrigerate for 1 to 2 hours. The onions are ready to eat once they are pinkish red.

2. Preheat the fire for direct cooking over medium-high heat (375°F, or 190.5°C). Place a Dutch oven over the fire for 3 to 4 minutes to preheat.

3. **To make the seasoning paste**: Place the chiles and garlic in the pot and let char for 30 to 45 seconds per side. Pour 2 cups (480 ml) of water into the pot and let simmer over the fire for 7 to 8 minutes. Remove the pot from the fire. Remove the chiles and garlic, discard the water, and wipe the pot clean. In a food processor, combine the chiles and garlic, oregano, agave, salt, cinnamon, and nutmeg. Add the remaining ¼ cup (60 ml) of water to the blender and blend until completely smooth. Pour the paste into a large bowl.

recipe continues

4. **To make the beef**: Place the Dutch oven over the fire again. Season the short ribs liberally with salt, pepper, and garlic powder and sear each side of the ribs until browned all over, working in batches, if needed. With the seared ribs in the Dutch oven, pour in the chile paste, broth, and beer. Cover the Dutch oven and simmer the beef over medium-high heat for 3½ to 4½ hours until the beef is fork-tender. Skim any fat from the top of the sauce, as needed.

5. Pull the beef off the bones and shred the meat. Discard the bones. Return the beef to the pot and mix it with the sauce. Set aside and keep warm.

6. **To make the tacos**: Heat a skillet on the fire over medium heat (325°F, or 163°C) and lightly toast the tortillas on each side. Build your tacos: spread a layer of sour cream on the tortillas, top with shredded beef, pickled red onion, Cotija cheese, and cilantro.

ANCHO COFFEE HANGING TOMAHAWKS WITH BLUE CHEESE SAUCE

I once had the pleasure of cooking with a slew of friends in Bryce Canyon National Park. While there, Chef David Olson and Matt Crawford, a.k.a. Sasquatch BBQ, hatched a plan to cook some tomahawk steaks hanging over an open fire. After breaking out the power tools, hanging these bad boys over the coals and watching them for an hour, the steaks were still only 100°F (38°C)—way too rare. Continuing to cook them while hanging risked compromising the quality of the steak, so I proposed taking them off the hangers and throwing them right into the coals! It worked like a dream and this hanging tomahawk steak recipe was born. Since then, I have recreated this recipe multiple times, with many flavor variations—this one is my favorite. The primarily bitter, but slightly sweet, ancho coffee rub amplifies the flavor from the coals. Served with a side of tangy blue cheese sauce, you've got the perfect recipe for any weekend warrior who wants to up their grilled meat game!

PREP TIME: 15 MINUTES | BRINE TIME: 1 HOUR | COOK TIME: 1 HOUR 45 MINUTES

Yield: 4 servings

FOR STEAKS

2 bone-in tomahawk rib eyes (with long bones)

Canola oil for coating the steaks

1 recipe Ancho Coffee Rub (page 40)

FOR BLUE CHEESE SAUCE

¼ cup (30 g) crumbled blue cheese

2 tablespoons (28 g) mayonnaise

2 tablespoons (30 ml) buttermilk

2 tablespoons (30 g) sour cream

1½ teaspoons garlic salt

SPECIAL GEAR

Metal tripod with chains, butcher twine, food-safe wire or a butcher hook

1. **To make the steaks**: Using a ¼-inch (0.6 cm) drill bit, drive a hole into the top part of the tomahawk steak bones. Using butcher twine, truss the tomahawks so they will hang over your fire, 5 to 6 inches (13 to 15 cm) from the coals.

2. Lather the steaks with oil and thoroughly season all sides, including the sides, of the steaks with the rub. Refrigerate, uncovered, for 1 hour to set.

3. Build a large fire in a fire pit and let it burn until the fire reaches medium to medium-high heat (about 350°F, or 180°C). Set up your tripod, or your own hanging device, over the pit.

4. Let the steaks sit at room temperature for 15 minutes, then hang the steaks over the fire and cook for 1 to 1½ hours until the internal temperature reaches between 105°F and 110°F (40.5°C and 43°C). Add charcoal and wood to maintain the temperature of the fire.

5. **To make the blue cheese sauce**: While the steaks cook, in a small bowl, stir together the blue cheese, mayonnaise, buttermilk, sour cream, and garlic salt. Refrigerate until needed.

recipe continues

6. **To finish the steaks**: When the steaks are close to hitting temperature, get your fire built with lots of white-hot charcoal, or preheat a charcoal chimney, if you like. Blow off the loose ash, pull the steaks off the tripod, and lay them directly into the coals. Cook for 4 to 5 minutes, flipping the steaks about every minute, until they reach an internal temperature of 120°F (49°C) for medium-rare. Pull the steaks off the coals and let rest for 7 to 8 minutes.

7. Serve with the blue cheese sauce on the side.

Grill Marks or Crust: The Great Debate

When it comes to cooking over fire, there seems to be a debate about grill marks versus crust. Let me settle this quickly: it's all about preference! Although I tend to be a crust guy, I can understand the appeal of grill marks. For me, grill marks do not add as much flavor as a crust; however, they do indicate a steak cooked with precision. Getting pristine grill marks is not an easy task and they demonstrate that the steak you are eating was cooked with intention—from seasoning to the clean crosshatch marks on the meat. On the other hand, a crispy crust on the outside of a tender steak elevates the overall texture, which along with the browning of the meat, creates a delicious bite. And although I might be a crust guy, you are welcome to enjoy your steak however you like it!

COAL-ROASTED HANGER STEAKS WITH THAI CHILI SAUCE

The steak cut used here may be an unfamiliar one, and cooking on coals may be out of the average griller's comfort zone—so, you might be quick to dismiss this recipe. Before you do, I love to point out that almost everyone's "favorite" recipe was, at one point, out of their comfort zone in some way, and these coal-roasted hanger steaks could be your next new favorite. Holding a nice salty taste from the dry brine, this tender steak and amazing crust is sure to impress. The crust adds subtle bitter flavor from the charcoal but it's balanced by the sour and spicy sauce. This recipe is perfect to share on a date night or with a group of adventurous friends looking to expand their palates.

PREP TIME: 20 MINUTES | BRINE TIME: 1 HOUR | COOK TIME: 15 MINUTES

Yield: 4 servings

FOR SEASONING
1½ tablespoons (27 g) coarse sea salt
1½ tablespoons (12.75 g) black peppercorns
1½ tablespoons (15 g) dried minced garlic
2 teaspoons red pepper flakes

FOR STEAKS
3 hanger steaks
1 tablespoon (15 ml) canola oil
2 lemons or limes, halved

FOR THAI CHILI SAUCE
2½ tablespoons (38 ml) fish sauce
2 tablespoons (20 g) minced garlic
1½ tablespoons (23 g) Thai chili paste
1½ tablespoons (23 ml) white wine vinegar
1 tablespoon (1 g) chopped fresh cilantro
1 tablespoon (g) chopped scallion, green parts only
Juice of 2 limes
Juice of 1 lemon

SPECIAL GEAR
Cast-iron skillet
Mortar and pestle

1. **To make the seasoning**: Using a mortar and pestle, crush the salt, peppercorns, garlic, and red pepper flakes into a medium grind.

2. **To make the steaks**: Lather the steaks with the oil and coat thoroughly with the seasoning. Refrigerate, uncovered, for at least 1 hour, ideally overnight.

3. Thirty minutes before cooking, remove the steaks from the refrigerator and let them come to room temperature.

4. Preheat the grill for cooking on the coals over high heat (400°F, or 200°C).

5. **To make the Thai chili sauce**: While the grill preheats, in a small bowl, stir together all the sauce ingredients.

6. Just before adding the steaks to the coals, blow off any loose ash from the coals. Place the steaks on the coals and cook for 2 to 3 minutes per side, or until the internal temperature reaches 120°F (49°C) and they have a good crust. Pull the steaks off the coals and let rest for 7 to 8 minutes.

7. While the steaks rest, place a cast-iron skillet or grill grate over the coals. Place the lemon halves in the skillet, cut-side down, and char for 3 to 4 minutes until blackened.

8. Slice the steaks against the grain and serve with the sauce and charred lemons on the side for squeezing.

Roasted Garlic Bomb

If you have ever been to a super swanky steakhouse, you might have been served roasted garlic bombs with your steak. I never understood why they did this—was it just a weird garnish? Truth is, these bombs are the greatest gift you can add to a meal. Roasted next to the fire at high heat, these smoky garlic bulbs equal a flavor bomb for just about any cut of meat, or anything, really. The key is to use a really sharp knife to slice off just the top of the garlic head to expose the cloves underneath without cutting off too much of the garlic itself. Roasted for about 45 minutes, you get a savory garlic paste with a hint of smoke from the fire. These are best served over a steak, added to a finishing sauce, mixed into your chimichurri or flavored butter, or just spread over some toast. You will thank me later.

PREP TIME: 10 MINUTES | COOK TIME: 45 MINUTES

Yield: 2 servings

2 or 3 whole garlic heads
2 teaspoons canola oil
1 teaspoon coarse sea salt
1 teaspoon freshly ground
   black pepper
1 teaspoon red pepper flakes

SPECIAL GEAR
None

1. Peel off some of the loose outer layers of skin from the garlic bulbs. Carefully slice off the top of each bulb to expose the tops of the cloves. Lather the exposed cloves with oil and season with salt, pepper, and red pepper flakes. Wrap each bulb in aluminum foil and set aside.

2. Preheat the grill for two-zone indirect cooking over high heat (400°F, or 200°C).

3. Place the wrapped garlic heads on the cool side of the grill and roast for 30 to 45 minutes until the garlic is soft to the touch and the heads have browned. Pull the garlic off the grill and let cool for 1 to 2 minutes.

4. For serving, carefully press the cloves out of their skins. They will be very paste-like.

ITALIAN HERB BUTTER ROTISSERIE PRIME RIB

You can't write a great grilling and barbecue cookbook without a prime rib recipe. I think this Italian herb butter rotisserie prime rib is everything you want a prime rib to taste like and more! The combination of a salty butter mixture and the assertive savory garlic taste takes the meat to another level. Using a rotisserie gives you that incredible crust—just be sure to cook it slowly using the classic rotisserie method. This will help prevent flare-ups and result in a more even cook.

PREP TIME: 30 MINUTES | BRINE TIME: 2 HOURS | COOK TIME: 2½ HOURS

Yield: 4 servings

FOR PRIME RIB

1 bone-in or boneless prime rib roast (preferably 4 bones)

Canola oil for coating the prime rib

¼ cup (56 g) OTFC All-Purpose Beef Rub (page 39)

FOR ITALIAN HERB BUTTER

3 cups (6 sticks, or 672 g) unsalted butter, at room temperature

2½ tablespoons (21 g) garlic paste

1 tablespoon (1.7 g) fresh rosemary leaves, chopped

2 teaspoons fresh thyme leaves, chopped

2 tablespoons (5 g) chopped fresh sage

2 teaspoons kosher salt

2 tablespoons (12 g) freshly ground black pepper

1 tablespoon (5.6 g) red pepper flakes

SPECIAL GEAR

Aluminum foil pan or cast-iron skillet, rotisserie with prongs, basting skillet

1. **To prepare the prime rib**: Lather the prime rib with oil and season it thoroughly with the rub. Refrigerate, uncovered, for 1 to 2 hours.

2. Preheat a three-zone fire for rotisserie cooking, with the rotisserie between the two fires, over medium heat (325°F, or 163°C). Place an aluminum foil pan or cast-iron skillet between the two fires to catch the rotisserie drippings, and add wood or charcoal throughout the cook to maintain the temperature, as needed.

3. Pull the meat from the refrigerator and skewer and secure it to the rotisserie. Place the prime rib over the fire and turn on the rotisserie. Cook for about 2½ hours until the internal temperature reaches 120°F (49°C), being alert for flare-ups. Do not be afraid to pull the meat away from the heat to let the fire cool.

4. **To make the herb butter**: About 10 minutes before the prime rib is done, place a basting skillet over the fire and add the butter, garlic, herbs, salt, pepper, and red pepper flakes. Cook until the butter is melted and the ingredients are blended. Set aside.

5. Pull the prime rib off the fire and let it rest for 10 minutes. Before slicing and serving, lather the prime rib with the herb butter.

A Breakdown of Beef and Its Grading

When it comes to beef and grading, the United States Department of Agriculture (USDA) has created a uniform scale that evaluates meat based on its tenderness, juiciness, and flavor. This helps you make the best choices for the best quality beef when cooking. When it comes to grading, the distinguishing factor among the grades is the meat's fat marbling—the white fat you find between the muscle fibers of the beef. This fat greatly affects the meat's tenderness, juiciness, and flavor! Here is a quick look at the three most common beef grades you'll see at a local grocery store or butcher shop in the United States.

USDA Select: "Select" identifies leaner, less fatty beef. This meat is appropriate for all kinds of cooking over fire. Select cuts tend to be cost efficient as well. You can tenderize the meat by braising it, or brining or marinating it before cooking.

USDA Choice: "Choice" beef is a step above Select beef in marbling, but does not have quite the fattiness of Prime beef. Choice beef is the most common selection of meat at your grocery store or butcher shop, with standard pricing. Choice beef is the classic marbled steak that loves the barbecue and grill.

USDA Prime: "Prime" is the highest grade of USDA-evaluated beef. It is highly marbled, tender, juicy, and flavorful—prime (pun intended) for grilling over the flames. And although Prime cuts might be pricey, they are worth it for special occasions.

In addition to the USDA grades, there are some industry terms used to explain beef beyond these three labels:

Grass fed: Grass-fed beef comes from an animal that only eats grass or foraged food in its lifetime, as opposed to eating grain or grain products. Grass-fed beef tends to have a distinctively darker color, yellow fat, and a slightly "beefier" flavor.

Grain finished: Most cattle are raised on a pasture eating grass or foraging for food. However, what cattle eat for the last period of their life can greatly affect their meat's flavor. So, you have cattle that are finished on grain to richen the flavor of the meat and give it a nice fat marbling.

Kobe: Kobe is a specific cattle breed inside the Japanese Wagyu cattle family. It is highly prized and must be traced back in origin to be considered true Kobe beef. Vet your Kobe beef for authenticity, as many sellers claim the name without the proof.

Wagyu: This is a breed of cattle from Japan (although other countries are now raising Wagyu cattle) with a high amount of intramuscular fat and marbling, which translates to tenderness and flavor. It is a highly prized (and expensive) cut of beef with its own grading scale outside of the USDA scale.

GREEN CHILE AND BACON CHEESEBURGERS

My time living in West Texas reshaped my opinion about food, people, and culture for the better. And, being so close to New Mexico, my friends and I would go to Ruidoso after a good winter storm to ski and snowboard. One of my first times there, the ski lodge rolled out these huge grills and made green chile burgers. Salty, savory, spicy, with a little tanginess right at the end to keep you wanting more. That memory lives on in this recipe.

PREP TIME: 20 MINUTES | COOK TIME: 15 MINUTES

Yield: 4 servings

FOR BURGER PATTIES

1½ pounds (681 g) ground beef chuck (preferably 85/15)

8 bacon slices, halved widthwise

2 teaspoons kosher salt

2 teaspoons freshly ground black pepper

2 teaspoons garlic powder

4 slices Monterey Jack cheese

4 burger buns

1½ tablespoons (21 g) unsalted butter, at room temperature

2 tablespoons (28 g) mayonnaise

FOR GREEN CHILE SAUCE

1½ tablespoons (23 ml) canola oil

1 tablespoon (10 g) finely chopped white onion

1 tablespoon (10 g) minced garlic

1 cup (180 g) roasted green chiles

1½ teaspoons chopped fresh cilantro

1½ teaspoons kosher salt

Juice of 1 lime

SPECIAL GEAR

Cast-iron skillet

1. **To start the cheeseburgers**: Place the ground beef in the freezer for 5 minutes. Then, form the beef into about four ⅓-pound (151 g) burger patties, making sure not to overhandle the meat. Make a slight indent in the center of each patty, so they do not bubble up on the grill. Refrigerate the patties until you are ready to cook.

2. Preheat the grill for direct cooking over medium-high heat (375°F, or 190.5°C). Place a cast-iron skillet over the fire about 2 minutes before cooking.

3. **To make the green chile sauce**: Pour the oil into the skillet and add the onion. Let sweat for 2 minutes, stirring frequently. Once the onion begins to brown, add the garlic and green chiles. Simmer for 2 to 3 minutes, then transfer the vegetables to a medium bowl and let cool. Stir in the cilantro, salt, and lime juice. Set aside. Clean the skillet.

4. **To finish the cheeseburgers**: With the grill still set up for direct grilling over medium-high heat (375°F, or 190.5°C), return the skillet to the grill to preheat.

5. Place the bacon in the hot skillet and cook it to your preferred doneness. Remove the skillet and bacon from the grill.

6. Season the burger patties on both sides with the salt, pepper, and garlic powder. Place the patties directly on the grill and cook for 3 to 4 minutes per side until they reach an internal temperature of 160°F (71°C). Top each burger with 1 slice of cheese and let it melt. Pull the patties from the grill and keep warm.

7. Spread the butter on the cut sides of your buns and lightly toast them over the fire.

8. **Build your burgers**: spread some mayo on the bottom bun, add 1 or 2 burger patties, bacon, green chile sauce, a top bun, and enjoy!

BLACK GARLIC NEW YORK STRIPS WITH BONE MARROW BUTTER

When doing research for this cookbook, I had the pleasure of talking recipes with friends, family, and colleagues and, although my name is listed as author, it was definitely a team effort! This recipe is a good example. I was developing beef recipes when a chat about flavor with my good friend Brad Prose (@chilesandsmoke) came around to black garlic. Not only is black garlic delicious, but it also brings an extra umami burst to the flavors as well. For this recipe, we blend black garlic into a powder, then remix the classic SPG (salt, pepper, and garlic) trio with the black garlic powder instead of regular garlic powder. Top it all off with an herbal, salty bone marrow butter, and you have steak paradise. This is a recipe to impress.

PREP TIME: 20 MINUTES, PLUS OVERNIGHT TO SOAK | BRINE TIME: 1 HOUR | COOK TIME: 15 MINUTES

Yield: 4 servings

FOR BONE MARROW

4 center-cut beef bones

2 tablespoons (30 g) kosher salt

2 gallons (7.6 L) water

FOR STEAK

3 black garlic cloves, peeled

2 teaspoons kosher salt

2 teaspoons freshly ground black pepper

3 New York strip steaks

1 tablespoon (15 ml) canola oil

Chopped fresh chives for garnish

Coarse sea salt for finishing

FOR BONE MARROW SEASONING

1 teaspoon chopped fresh rosemary leaves

1 teaspoon chopped fresh thyme leaves

1 teaspoon black peppercorns

1 teaspoon dried minced garlic

1 teaspoon coarse sea salt

SPECIAL GEAR

Food processor, mortar and pestle

1. **To make the bone marrow:** The night before cooking, in a very large bowl or food-safe container, combine the water and kosher salt, stirring to dissolve the salt. Add the beef bones and refrigerate overnight to extract any impurities from the bones.

2. **To make the steaks:** In a food processor or spice grinder, process the black garlic until you have a powder. Put the powder through a fine-mesh sieve to remove any lumps. In a small bowl, stir together 2 teaspoons of black garlic powder, the kosher salt, and pepper. Lather the steaks with oil and season all sides with SPG. Refrigerate the steaks, uncovered, for at least 1 hour, ideally 4, to dry brine.

3. **To make the bone marrow seasoning:** Using a mortar and pestle, grind the rosemary, thyme, peppercorns, garlic, and sea salt until coarse. Set aside.

recipe continues

4. Remove the bones from the water and pat dry. Discard the water.

5. Remove the steaks from the refrigerator and let them and the bones sit at room temperature for 15 minutes.

6. Preheat the grill for direct cooking over high heat (400°F, or 200°C).

7. **To cook the steaks**: Place the steaks on the grill and cook for 2 to 3 minutes per side, or until the internal temperature reaches 120°F (49°C). Remove the steaks from the grill and let rest, covered, for 8 to 10 minutes.

8. **To finish the bone marrow**: While the steaks rest, place the bones on the grill, open-side down. Cook for 3 to 4 minutes, flip, and cook for 2 to 3 minutes more until the bone marrow is bubbling and liquefying. Remove from the grill and let cool for 1 minute. Sprinkle the bones with the bone marrow seasoning.

9. Slice the steaks, top with a scoop of bone marrow from the bones, and garnish with fresh chives and sea salt.

SPICED RUM–MARINATED TRI-TIP

Beautifully cooked jerk chicken is something not to be missed and this spiced rum-marinated tri-tip is inspired by the thing I love about jerk chicken: that signature marinade. Jerk marinade is a blend of spicy peppers, specifically Scotch bonnets, with savory and spiced notes, and more. Combining that flavorful mix with spiced rum seemed like a no-brainer. The biggest shift was using beef instead of chicken—and figuring out the perfect cut, which I find to be tri-tip, since I often marinate before cooking it slowly over the coals. The last piece was adding a sweet but spicy barbecue sauce for dipping! This is an awesome party meal served with plantains, rice, or any kind of potatoes.

PREP TIME: 20 MINUTES | MARINATE TIME: 4 HOURS | COOK TIME: 15 MINUTES

Yield: 4 to 6 servings

FOR SPICED RUM MARINADE

¼ cup (60 ml) white vinegar

½ cup (120 ml) soy sauce

½ cup (120 ml) spiced rum, plus more as needed

12 garlic cloves, peeled

3 tablespoons (30 g) chopped sweet onion

3 tablespoons (18 g) chopped scallion, green parts only

2 tablespoons (30 g) ginger paste

1 tablespoon (15 ml) canola oil

4 teaspoons (24 g) fine sea salt

4 teaspoons (8 g) freshly ground black pepper

4 teaspoons (20 g) brown sugar

2 teaspoons dried thyme

2 teaspoons ground cinnamon

2 teaspoons ground allspice

1 teaspoon ground nutmeg

2 or 3 Scotch bonnet peppers or habaneros, seeded

FOR STEAK

4 tablespoons (½ stick, or 56 g) unsalted butter

2 whole tri-tips

Chopped fresh cilantro for garnish

Lime wedges for serving

FOR BARBECUE SAUCE

½ cup (120 g) ketchup

¼ cup (60 ml) Spiced Rum Marinade

3 tablespoons (45 ml) apple cider vinegar

1 tablespoon (20 g) honey

SPECIAL GEAR

Basting skillet

1. **To make the marinade**: In a food processor, combine all the marinade ingredients, adding just 1 habanero at a time to test the heat level, which will reduce slightly when cooked. Blend to a thick paste, adding more rum if you like a thinner marinade. Reserve ½ cup (120 ml) of marinade.

2. **To make the steak**: Place the tri-tips in a large bowl and pour in the remaining marinade. Turn the beef to coat thoroughly in the marinade, then refrigerate for at least 4 hours, ideally overnight.

3. Preheat the grill for direct cooking over medium-high heat (350°F, or 180°C).

4. Place a basting skillet on the grill and add the butter to melt. Place ¼ cup of the reserved marinade in a small bowl and set aside for the barbecue sauce. Stir the remaining ¼ cup of reserved marinade into the butter. Use this marinade for basting in step 5. Move the skillet to the cool side of the grill to keep warm.

recipe continues

5. Remove the tri-tips from the marinade and place them on the grill. Discard the used marinade. Cook for 5 to 6 minutes, then baste with a bit of the butter and reserved marinade and flip the tri-tips. Cook for 20 to 25 minutes more, basting and flipping about every 5 minutes, until the outside of the tri-tips is well crusted and the internal temperature reaches 125°F (52°C) for medium-rare. Remove the steaks and let rest for 10 minutes

6. **To make the barbecue sauce**: While the steaks rest, in a medium bowl, stir together the barbecue sauce ingredients.

7. Slice the steak against the grain, garnish with fresh cilantro, and serve with lime wedges for squeezing and the sauce on the side.

When to Salt Your Steak

The key to knowing when to salt your steak is understanding dry brining. Dry brining is similar to wet brining in that it uses salt and moisture to create a more concentrated meat flavor and prevent moisture loss during cooking. Dry brining also adds great overall flavor as the salt is reabsorbed into the meat and retains its flavor. The main difference between wet and dry brining is that dry brining does not use added moisture, only the meat's natural moisture to create the brine. In short, dry brining is seasoning a protein, in this case steak, with salt and letting it sit for a period of time (usually in the refrigerator). So, instead of asking when to salt your steak, ask how long you should dry brine your steak. I think the best answer is to dry brine your steak for at least 45 minutes to 1 hour before you grill it. This will produce a great outside crust and delicious flavor. If you have the time, dry brining for between 4 and 24 hours gives you the most intense flavor possible. If you do not have a ton of time, seasoning right before you cook over the flames is okay. Make the best of your steak with the time you have!

PINEAPPLE BOURBON STEAK TIPS

Tim Van Doren is a long-time barbecue cook and social media influencer revealing the inner world of steak competitions. You can say he has mastered how to make steak! One of my favorite recipes of his is called Steak Maui. It is an ode to Hawaiian and Pacific Island flavors. My big take-away from him is the use of pineapple juice in the marinade. The unique properties in pineapple, from a digestive enzyme called bromelain that breaks down amino acids, can make just about any cut of meat more tender and delicious, and that is the basis for these steak tips. By cutting tough sirloin into cubes, you increase the surface area for the marinade to work and to absorb even more pineapple bourbon sauce goodness—a bit savory, sweet, and full of Hawaiian flavors. Cooking in a skillet gives you the most amazing crust on these steak tips because of the sugar in the marinade. Serve this steak with some warm rice, asparagus, or a nice salad (yes, salad) for a great weeknight meal.

PREP TIME: 15 MINUTES | MARINATE TIME: 2 HOURS | COOK TIME: 10 MINUTES

Yield: 4 servings

FOR PINEAPPLE BOURBON MARINADE

1 cup (240 ml) low-sodium soy sauce

½ cup (120 ml) unsweetened pineapple juice

¼ cup (60 ml) rice wine vinegar

¼ cup (60 ml) bourbon or whiskey

2½ tablespoons (38 g) brown sugar

2 tablespoons (28 g) garlic paste

1½ tablespoons (23 g) ginger paste

2 teaspoons canola oil

1 teaspoon sesame oil

FOR STEAK

1½ pounds (681 g) sirloin tips, cubed

1 tablespoon (15 ml) canola oil

2 tablespoons (28 g) unsalted butter

Toasted sesame seeds for garnish

Chopped scallion, green parts only, for garnish

SPECIAL GEAR

Large cast-iron skillet or wok

1. **To make the pineapple bourbon marinade:** In a large bowl, stir together all the marinade ingredients.

2. **To make the steak:** Carefully, add the cubed steak tips to the marinade and mix thoroughly. Refrigerate to marinate for at least 2 hours, ideally overnight.

3. Preheat the grill for direct cooking over high heat (400°F, or 200°C).

4. Pour the oil into a cast-iron skillet or wok and place it over the flames for 1 to 2 minutes to preheat.

5. Remove the steak from the marinade and discard the marinade. Working in two or three batches, add the steak to the hot skillet, being sure not to overcrowd it. Cook for about 2 minutes, making sure to get a nice golden-brown crust on the steak, before flipping and cooking for 2 to 3 minutes more until the internal temperature is about 120°F (49°C). Transfer the steak to a serving bowl, top with the butter, and let rest for 5 minutes.

6. Before serving, mix the melted butter into the steaks. Garnish with sesame seeds and scallion.

3
PORK

Pork is the favorite of many when cooking over fire. From traditional Southern barbecue to Southeast Asian cuisine, there are many well-known dishes that feature pork. Yet, that doesn't mean pork is easy to cook: Many people do not understand the basics of pork and how to best cook it. Once you crack the code, though, with just a few tips and tricks, pork is easy.

First, you need to be careful because pork has a lot of fat; I mean A LOT of fat. Look no further than bacon, which is cured and smoked pork belly. It is one of my favorite things—in fact, bacon (and fat in general) makes everything better. Wrap it, bake it, candy it, smoke it, or just cook it. Bacon can make many dishes go from average to out of this world. It also teaches us the first lesson: bacon can burn very fast because it gives off a lot of greasy fat. So, although pork fat is generally our friend, it can also be a nemesis if you don't tend your fire temperature well.

Second, pork can sometimes take time to cook and render that fat, which is why you will find a lot of recipes in this chapter that take 6 to 7 hours to cook. Pork ribs, pork butt, and even pork belly must be cooked slowly, at low temperatures, to break down all that fat and make the meat super tender. There are quicker recipes, too, like for pork tenderloin or pork chops. But in general, cooking pork can take time, so plan accordingly.

Last, pork adds a ton of savory salty flavor to almost any dish. If you need a burst of savoriness or want to amp up the fat in a lean cut of meat, use bacon, fry it in lard, or otherwise add some pork fat. Using pork fat this way can also take many leaner meats, such as venison, elk, chicken, or even beef into another flavor level. Do not be afraid to level up your flavor game!

PORK AND TASTE

When it comes to different tastes, pork is versatile. It can be used with just about any combination—salty, sour, bitter, sweet, or umami—and be absolutely delicious! The key is to cook the pork in the ideal way, so the specific tastes are accentuated.

Salty

You want to add salt to just about any meat, and pork is no exception. Be careful, though, that you do not oversalt your pork, as pork has a natural salty savory taste. The salty flavor can be overpowering if you add heavy amounts of salt onto cuts such as pork belly, ribs, and more. This does not mean to leave out the salt; just use restraint.

Sour

The way I like to use sour in my pork recipes is from vinegar. Because pork is so fatty, vinegar can help "cut" the fat, producing a more well-rounded flavor profile on the pork. I love to use vinegar in my spritz on pork ribs. This creates a nice crust but also makes a great base layer of tartness for an already fatty, salty, and sweet dish.

Bitter

There are many ways to add bitterness to pork that make a big impact. Coffee is my favorite way to get that bitter taste combination on my pork chops, pork loin, or pork roasts. Coffee has a mild bitter flavor that turns slightly sweet when you begin to cook it. The bitter in coffee is a great addition to pork marinades, glazes, or seasonings because it complements pork's natural saltiness and combines for a very robust dish. Try using coffee as a spritz as well for your pork to get a darker crust with a hint of sweetness.

Sweet

This is the primary taste I like with pork! Because of pork's inherently salty/savory taste, adding sweet boosts those tastes and makes them pop. You can experience this effect in barbecues, specifically. I love to use sweeteners like brown sugar, honey, molasses, or even agave on pork shoulder, pork ribs, and roasts. The sweetener creates a caramelized crust on the outside of the meat while providing a simple sweetness to the taste.

Umami/Savory

For pork, umami/savory flavor is a part of everything. As I already mentioned, you can add bacon to other cuts of meat to amp up the umami savoriness. This is an easy and effective way to take your food to the next level! For example, pork tenderloin is delicious wrapped in bacon. The bacon adds fat to a relatively lean cut of meat while keeping that savory punch. Another way to amp up pork with umami is with soy sauce or fish sauce used as a marinade, glaze, or more to bring out that good pork flavor.

PORK AND FLAVOR

When it comes to flavor for pork, using every piece of the flavor puzzle adds to it. Remember, flavor is the combination of taste, aroma, temperature, texture, and experience. This combination helps create the overall picture for each dish but that is unique to each individual one. We will not all experience these pork recipes the same way, and you might even change pieces of a recipe to fit what you enjoy, and that is fine!

Aroma

If you've ever woken to the smell of bacon cooking, you know how enticing heat plus pork can be. You will notice that with pork, adding sweet creates a smell while cooking over the fire that is rich, sweet, and smoky, and the pork will absorb a lot of that smoke flavor from the fire. And, that initial aroma is one of pork's biggest benefits because it will tell you if you're doing something wrong. Because of the fat and sugar, watch your fire temperature and be aware of any burning or rancid aromas.

Temperature/Heat

When it comes to spiciness and pork, fresh chiles instead of dried chiles tend to be the better choice. The spiciness of fresh chiles, such as jalapeño, serrano, and Thai chiles, when mixed with sour tastes, like lime juice and vinegar, cuts through the pork fat better and the taste of the chiles still shines. That said, dried chiles, like chipotle and guajillo, are very good with slowly braised or smoked pork. When you amplify the smokiness of the chiles with the smoke from the grill on the pork, you have an amazing flavor combination.

Texture

As with any meat, some pork cuts are tender and some are tough. For the recipes here, I focus on pork becoming very tender with lots of moisture when cooked right. Pulled pork, pork belly, and pork ribs should fall apart in your mouth from their tenderness. Pork tenderloin and pork chops should not be the exception to this rule. You will find many leaner cuts of pork have plenty of tenderness, especially when brined, marinated, and cooked slowly.

Experience

For me, pork is a comfort food—a food you want for lunch on your day off from work, or the meat you hope to enjoy at the end of the day with your family around the table. Whether you are making pulled pork sandwiches or glazing a ham for the holidays, pork can be the star of a party or something you can enjoy by yourself. I urge you to see pork as more than just bacon or ribs. It creates memories for those who gather with it at the center of their table.

PORK AND FIRE

When it comes to what fire can do for pork, we need to review direct and indirect cooking. When direct cooking pork, you tend to get a nice crust because of how delicious pork fat is when rendered. Pork chops and tenderloin are classic direct cooking cuts that develop a beautiful crust. Pork fat, though, is saltier and sweeter in nature than beef fat, so you need to watch for too much charring and the resulting bitterness, which can occur quickly. The char created on pork by direct cooking does not create that same pleasant bitterness it does on steak. Pork fat also has a lower smoke point than beef fat or vegetable oil, so you must watch your fire temperature to prevent burning. When you do get that nice crust on pork, though, the smokiness from the flames brings out that subtle sweetness in pork unlike anything else.

As for indirect cooking, pork is a staple meat for classic Southern barbecue. Baby back ribs, pulled pork, and even ham are ideal for the smoker because pork absorbs so much smokiness while still being a canvas of flavor. When you smoke pork with salty seasoning and slather it in sweet barbecue sauce you are bound to fall in love with the results. The subtle natural sweet saltiness of pork amplifies that tender meat from the smoker. Most cuts of pork cooked indirectly take multiple hours to break down that fat slowly, but you are left with juicy, fall-off-the-bone meat, combining taste, flavor, and fire: hog heaven.

COTIJA-CRUSTED PORK SKEWERS

For years, I used to go to Rodizio Grill Brazilian Steakhouse in downtown Nashville to celebrate my birthday. This recipe is an ode to my favorite dish there as well as their amazing chefs and staff. Marinated in a savory chile marinade, these pork loin steaks are skewered and cooked over the fire, then coated with a nice salty Cotija cheese crust. This packs a delicious punch and creates a gooey crust.

PREP TIME: 30 MINUTES | MARINATE TIME: 4 HOURS | COOK TIME: 20 MINUTES

Yield: 4 servings

FOR MARINADE

2 dried guajillo chiles, stemmed and seeded

2 dried ancho chiles, stemmed and seeded

4 garlic cloves, peeled

2 cups (480 ml) water, plus 2 tablespoons (30 ml)

½ cup (120 ml) white vinegar

¼ cup (60 ml) soy sauce

1 tablespoon (7 g) ground cinnamon

1 tablespoon (15 g) kosher salt

1 tablespoon (3 g) dried oregano

1½ tablespoons (23 ml) canola oil

FOR PORK

½ whole pork loin, trimmed

½ cup (56 g) grated Cotija cheese

¼ cup (4 g) chopped fresh cilantro

SPECIAL GEAR

Dutch oven, skewers

1. Preheat the fire/grill for direct grilling over medium-high heat (375°F, or 190.5°C). Place a Dutch oven over the fire for 3 to 4 minutes to preheat.

2. **To make the marinade:** Place the chiles and garlic in the pot and let char for 30 to 45 seconds per side. Pour 2 cups (480 ml) of water into the pot and let simmer over the fire for 7 to 8 minutes. Remove the pot from the fire. Remove the chiles and garlic, discard the water, and wipe the pot clean. In a food processor, combine the chiles and garlic, vinegar, soy sauce, cinnamon, salt, oregano, and remaining 2 tablespoons (30 ml) of water. Blend until smooth. Pour the marinade into a large bowl.

3. **To make the pork:** Slice the pork loin lengthwise down the middle, then slice each side into 2-inch (5 cm)-thick steaks. Place the pork steaks into the marinade and mix thoroughly. Refrigerate to marinate for 4 hours, ideally overnight.

4. Remove the pork from the marinade and discard the marinade. Thread the pork steaks onto skewers, with the fat cap facing out, so it can render.

5. Preheat the fire for direct cooking over medium-high heat (375°F, or 190.5°C) and wait for the fire to become coals to prevent flare-ups.

6. Place the skewers over the fire and cook for 7 to 8 minutes per side until the internal temperature of the pork reaches about 145°F (63°C).

7. Right before the pork is done, pull the skewers off the fire and cover the pork on both sides with the Cotija cheese. Return the skewers to the grill and cook over the coals for 30 to 60 seconds to caramelize the crust. Pull the skewers off the fire and let rest for 2 to 3 minutes. Serve garnished with fresh cilantro.

3-2-1 SMOKED RIBS WITH HONEY PEPPERCORN BBQ SAUCE

If you are new to cooking with fire, you might not be familiar with the 3-2-1 method of cooking pork ribs. This is a classic barbecue technique for producing "foolproof" tender ribs that doesn't break a sweat. The name, 3-2-1, describes the process: 3-hour smoke at 250°F (121°C) with only seasoning, followed by a 2-hour smoked in an aluminum foil/butter wrap, and finished with a 1-hour smoke lathered in sauce. The key is controlling temperature. Sugar and butter begin to burn if you get too close to 350°F (180°C), so regulate your pit's temperature the whole time! This is a classic recipe, with a few Derek Wolf–style twists, for the most authentic flavor. A nice salty barbecue seasoning gets things started and the sauce is plenty sweet and spicy. This is a crowd favorite at my house.

PREP TIME: 20 MINUTES | BRINE TIME: 2 HOURS | COOK TIME: 6 HOURS

Yield: 4 servings

FOR SEASONING

1 tablespoon (15 g) brown sugar

2 teaspoons chipotle chile powder

2 teaspoons garlic powder

2 teaspoons freshly ground black pepper

2 teaspoons fine sea salt

1½ teaspoons smoked paprika

1 teaspoon onion powder

FOR SPRITZ

1 cup (240 ml) apple cider vinegar

2 teaspoons hot sauce

FOR RIBS

3 whole slabs baby back pork ribs

1½ tablespoons (23 g) spicy mustard

FOR CRUTCH

1 cup plus 2 tablespoons (2 sticks plus 2 tablespoons, or 252 g) unsalted butter

6 tablespoons (90 g) brown sugar

3 tablespoons (60 g) honey

FOR HONEY PEPPERCORN BBQ SAUCE

¼ cup (60 ml) dark beer

½ cup (120 g) ketchup

¼ cup (60 ml) apple cider vinegar

2 tablespoons (40 g) honey

1 tablespoon (18 g) fine sea salt

2 teaspoons hot sauce

1½ teaspoons black peppercorns, freshly cracked

SPECIAL GEAR

Spritz bottle, basting skillet

1. **To make the seasoning**: In a small bowl, stir together all the seasoning ingredients.

2. **To make the spritz**: In a 16-ounce (480 ml) spray-top bottle, combine the vinegar and hot sauce. Cover and shake well.

3. **To make the ribs**: Carefully remove the membrane from the back of the ribs. Lather the ribs all over with the mustard and coat thoroughly with the seasoning. Refrigerate, uncovered, for 2 hours to set.

4. Preheat the smoker for indirect cooking over medium-low heat (250°F, or 121°C). Add some oak or hickory wood chunks or chips to the smoker for more smoke flavor.

5. Place the ribs in the smoker on the indirect heat side. Cook for 3 hours, spraying the ribs with the spritz every 30 minutes. Pull the ribs from the smoker.

recipe continues

6. **To make the crutch**: Place a piece of aluminum foil about 1½ times the length of the ribs on a work surface. Sprinkle 1 tablespoon (15 g) of brown sugar along the length of the foil. Drizzle ½ tablespoon (10 g) of honey along the foil over the brown sugar, and place 1 tablespoon (14 g) of butter in the middle of the foil and 1 tablespoon (14 g, times 2) of butter toward each end of the foil. Place one slab of ribs on the butter, bone-side up. Top the slab with 1 tablespoon (15 g) of brown sugar, ½ tablespoon (10 g) of honey, and 3 tablespoons (42 g) of butter in the same manner as underneath the ribs. Carefully wrap the foil around the ribs until tight and secure. Repeat this step with the remaining 2 slabs of ribs. Place the wrapped ribs back in the smoker, bone-side up. Cook for 2 hours.

7. **To make the sauce**: With 30 minutes left on the ribs, preheat a separate grill for direct cooking over medium-high heat (375°F, or 190.5°C). Place a basting skillet over the heat and pour in the beer. Cook for about 5 minutes until the beer reduces by half. Stir in the remaining sauce ingredients and simmer for 7 to 8 minutes until thickened. Pull the sauce off the heat.

8. **To finish the ribs**: After 2 hours, unwrap the ribs and discard the foil. Arrange the ribs in the smoker and increase the smoker's temperature to 350°F (180°C). Glaze the outside of the ribs with the sauce until completely covered. Cook the ribs for 20 to 25 minutes until they are caramelized and tender.

9. Pull the ribs off the fire and let rest for 3 to 5 minutes. Slice between the bones to serve.

Sweet Bourbon Mushrooms

The ultimate sweet and umami pairing for steak, pork ,or just about anything, I love adding caramelized mushrooms to my meals for a pop of sweet umami taste. The key for this recipe is adding the mushrooms to a skillet without any other ingredients to let them sweat. The mushrooms' moisture needs to evaporate to get that beautiful golden brown exterior. In fewer than 30 minutes, you will have an amazing side or topping!

PREP TIME: 15 MINUTES | COOK TIME: 15 MINUTES

Yield: Makes 1 cup

1 tablespoon (14 g) unsalted butter

2 cups (192 g) mushrooms, sliced

3 tablespoons (45 ml) bourbon

1 tablespoon (15 ml) balsamic vinegar

2 teaspoons soy sauce

½ teaspoon garlic powder

½ teaspoon sea salt

½ teaspoon freshly ground black pepper

SPECIAL GEAR

Cast-iron skillet

1. Preheat the fire for direct grilling over medium-high heat (350°F, or 180°C).

2. Put the butter in a cast-iron skillet and place it over the fire 2 minutes before cooking.

3. Add the mushrooms to the skillet and cook for 5 to 7 minutes, stirring occasionally, until the mushrooms release their liquid and it has evaporated and the mushrooms are golden brown.

4. Add the remaining ingredients and cook for 3 to 4 minutes until the liquids have reduced and thickened. Pull the skillet off the heat and serve.

GRILLED PORK CHOPS WITH GRAPEFRUIT BALSAMIC VINAIGRETTE

I think pork chops are so easy to overcook that it feels safer to avoid them all together. Well, not these pork chops. These chops are epic—delicious and super tender. The key: overnight brining, which tenderizes the meat, adds flavor, and helps keep the meat from becoming dry quickly. I pair these grilled chops, with their salty crust, with some bitter arugula and a drizzle of grapefruit balsamic vinaigrette, which gives a citrusy sweetness and a subtle bitter bite at the end.

PREP TIME: 30 MINUTES | BRINE TIME: 4 HOURS, OR OVERNIGHT | COOK TIME: 20 MINUTES

Yield: 4 servings

FOR BRINE

1 gallon (3.8 L) water

¼ cup (60 g) packed brown sugar

2½ tablespoons (38 g) kosher salt

2 bay leaves

FOR PORK

4 bone-in pork chops

1 tablespoon (15 ml) canola oil

2 cups (40 g) fresh arugula

FOR GRAPEFRUIT BALSAMIC VINAIGRETTE

Juice of 1 grapefruit

3 tablespoons (45 ml) balsamic vinegar

2 teaspoons chopped fresh rosemary leaves

2 teaspoons chopped fresh parsley

2 teaspoons chopped fresh thyme leaves

2 teaspoons kosher salt

1 teaspoon freshly ground black pepper

1 teaspoon brown sugar

2 tablespoons (30 ml) olive oil

FOR SEASONING

1½ teaspoons coarse sea salt

1½ teaspoons coarse black pepper

1 teaspoon dried minced garlic

1 teaspoon dried minced onion

1. **To make the brine**: Preheat a grill for direct cooking over medium-high heat (350°F, or 180°C) and place a saucepan over the fire (or on the stovetop). Pour in the water and add the brown sugar, salt, and bay leaves. Bring to a low boil and stir until the salt and sugar dissolve. Remove and let cool completely. Add ice, if needed, to help cool the water faster.

2. **To make the pork**: In a large food-safe container, combine the pork chops and cooled brine, making sure they are covered. Refrigerate for at least 4 hours, ideally up to 12 hours.

3. **To make the vinaigrette**: In a blender, combine the juice, vinegar, rosemary, parsley, thyme, salt, pepper, and brown sugar. Blend until smooth. Pour in the olive oil and blend until thickened. Transfer to an airtight container and refrigerate.

4. **To make the seasoning**: In a small bowl, stir together the salt, pepper, garlic, and onion.

5. **To finish the pork**: Remove the chops from the brine and pat dry. Discard the brine. Lather the chops with canola oil and thoroughly coat with the seasoning. Set aside.

6. Preheat the grill for direct cooking over medium-high heat (375°F, or 190.5°C).

7. Place the chops on the grill and cook for 4 to 5 minutes per side, or until the internal temperature reaches 145°F (63°C). Pull the chops off the fire and let rest for 2 to 3 minutes.

8. Serve the pork chops on a bed of arugula with the grapefruit balsamic vinaigrette drizzled on top.

CHILE CON LIMON CANDIED BACON

If you need another reason to love bacon, let me introduce you to candied bacon, the amped-up sibling of the bacon you already know and love. Cooked over low heat and covered in sugar, this chile con limon candied bacon is next level with its unique flavors. This candied bacon is one of a kind—first coated with a spicy tequila glaze to add sweetness to the savory bacon, followed by the sour kick from a homemade chile con limon seasoning—and it will make you forget you are even eating bacon. This is an awesome appetizer for any party or something to kick up your next Bloody Mary.

PREP TIME: 30 MINUTES | COOK TIME: 1 HOUR 15 MINUTES

Yield: 4 servings

FOR CHILE CON LIMON SEASONING

3 dried chiles (guajillo, chipotle, or other), seeded and chopped

3 tablespoons (28.2 g) citric acid

2 tablespoons (30 g) kosher salt

FOR SPICY TEQUILA GLAZE

2 tablespoons (30 ml) tequila

2 tablespoons (28 g) unsalted butter

¼ cup (80 g) agave nectar

2 teaspoons hot sauce (preferably cayenne-based)

FOR CANDIED BACON

12 bacon slices

3 tablespoons (45 g) brown sugar

5 teaspoons (20 g) Chile con Limon Seasoning, or store-bought seasoning

Fresh jalapeño slices for garnish

SPECIAL GEAR

Cast-iron skillet

1. Preheat the grill for direct cooking over medium-high heat (350°F, or 180°C).

2. **To make the seasoning:** In a blender, pulse the dried chiles into a powder. Transfer to a small bowl and stir in the citric acid and salt.

3. **To make the glaze:** Place a cast-iron skillet on the grill (or on a stovetop) and carefully pour in the tequila. Simmer for 1 to 1½ minutes, so the tequila reduces but does not evaporate completely. Stir in the remaining glaze ingredients and simmer for 3 to 4 minutes, stirring occasionally, until the glaze thickens. Remove from the heat and let cool for 5 minutes.

4. Preheat the smoker for indirect cooking over medium-low heat (275°F, or 135°C). Add some oak or cherrywood chunks or chips to the smoker for more smoke flavor.

5. **To make the candied bacon:** Lay the bacon slices on a baking sheet (preferably with a grate). Lather each slice with the spicy glaze, crumble half the brown sugar on top, and sprinkle with 2½ teaspoons of chile con limon seasoning.

6. Place the bacon in the smoker and cook for 25 to 35 minutes, or until the outside has begun to caramelize and the fat begins to render. Flip the bacon over and coat it with the glaze, crumble the remaining brown sugar on top, and sprinkle with the remaining 2½ teaspoons of seasoning. Cook for 25 to 35 minutes until caramelized.

7. Pull the bacon from the smoker and let cool for 5 to 10 minutes (don't skip this step; the bacon will be very hot!). Top with the jalapeños and enjoy!

COCOA MOLASSES–GLAZED SPIRAL HAM

Whether it's holiday time or just a fun dinner, smoking a spiral ham creates an amazing centerpiece for the meal. Because the ham is already cooked, it just needs some smoky flavor added and a cocoa molasses glaze, a blend of sweet and bitter tastes. Many hear cocoa and immediately think sweet. If you have ever had really dark chocolate, then you know cocoa is not sweet. The cocoa flavor lends a nice complementary bitter flavor to the sweet molasses. Pair that with the smokiness of the ham, and you have an amazing meal.

PREP TIME: 30 MINUTES | COOK TIME: 4 HOURS

Yield: 8 servings

FOR SEASONING

1 tablespoon (15 g) kosher salt

2 teaspoons freshly ground black pepper

2 teaspoons smoked paprika

2 teaspoons cocoa powder

1½ teaspoons garlic powder

1 teaspoon ground ginger

½ teaspoon cayenne pepper

FOR HAM

1 (about 8-pound, or 3.6 kg) spiral ham

2 (12-ounce, or 360 ml) bottles dark beer (preferably stout or porter)

FOR GLAZE

1 tablespoon (14 g) unsalted butter

2 tablespoons (30 g) ketchup

2 tablespoons (30 ml) water

2 tablespoons (40 g) molasses

1½ tablespoons (23 g) brown sugar

2 teaspoons cocoa powder

1½ teaspoons garlic powder

1½ teaspoons onion powder

SPECIAL GEAR

Cast-iron skillet

1. **To make the seasoning:** In a small bowl, stir together the seasoning ingredients.

2. **To make the ham:** Place the ham on a work surface, cut-side toward you. Thoroughly coat the ham with the seasoning, getting it into all the crevices. Set the ham aside until you are ready to cook.

3. Preheat the grill for indirect cooking over low heat (225°F, or 107°C). Add some cherrywood chips to the grill, if you want extra smoke flavor.

4. Place the ham on the grill and cook for about 1½ hours. Transfer the ham to a large aluminum foil pan and pour in the beer. Wrap the pan completely in foil and return it to the grill. Increase the temperature to 275°F (135°C) and cook for 2 to 2½ hours, or until the internal temperature reaches 145°F (63°C).

5. **To make the glaze:** When the ham is nearly done, preheat a grill for direct cooking over medium-high heat (350°F, or 180°C) and place a cast-iron skillet over the heat. Add the butter to melt, then stir in the remaining glaze ingredients. Mix thoroughly and simmer for 4 to 5 minutes until thickened.

6. **To finish the ham:** Remove the ham from the pan and place it on the grill. Discard the cooking liquid. Coat the ham on all sides with the glaze. Open all the vents on the grill to increase the heat level to high and let the heat caramelize the glaze. Cook for 7 to 8 minutes. Remove the ham from the heat and let rest for 5 minutes before slicing and serving.

PINEAPPLE TERIYAKI PULLED PORK SANDWICH

If you are a classic barbecue cook, you know about pulled pork! This is the magical cut of meat from the shoulder area of the pig (not the butt) but that is called a butt (that is a story for another time). Like brisket, it can be a beast to cook this meat as it has so much intermuscular fat that takes a long time to break down. However, with time and patience, it can be one of the best things you ever cook over fire, and this sandwich is no exception. With a simple seasoning, you will cook this cut for 8+ hours until it falls apart. It's finished with a sweet and savory pineapple teriyaki sauce for a fantastic meal that feeds lots of people on a summer (or any) evening.

PREP TIME: 1 HOUR | BRINE TIME: 4 HOURS | COOK TIME: 9 HOURS, PLUS 2 HOURS TO REST

Yield: 8 servings

FOR SEASONING
1½ tablespoons (23 g) brown sugar

1 tablespoon (15 g) kosher salt

2 teaspoons freshly ground black pepper

2 teaspoons garlic powder

1 teaspoon cayenne powder

FOR SPRITZ
½ cup (120 ml) apple cider vinegar

¼ cup (60 ml) pineapple juice

2 teaspoons hot sauce

FOR PORK
2 (10- to 12-pound, or 4.5 to 5.4 kg) bone-in pork butts

3 tablespoons (45 g) spicy mustard

8 hamburger buns

1½ tablespoons (23 ml) melted unsalted butter

FOR PINEAPPLE TERIYAKI SAUCE
⅓ cup (80 ml) soy sauce

⅓ cup (80 ml) pineapple juice

3 tablespoons (45 ml) water

1 tablespoon (8 g) cornstarch

3 tablespoons (45 g) brown sugar

1½ tablespoons (23 ml) rice wine vinegar

1 tablespoon (20 g) honey

2 teaspoons ginger paste

2 teaspoons garlic paste

SPECIAL GEAR
Spritz bottle, butcher paper, large cooler, cast-iron skillet

1. **To make the seasoning**: In a small bowl, stir together all the seasoning ingredients.

2. **To make the spritz**: In an 8-ounce (240 ml) spray bottle, combine all the spritz ingredients. Cover and shake well.

3. **To make the pork**: Remove the fat cap from the pork (save it for rendering) and clean out the sinew in the flap of the meat. Lather each pork butt with half the mustard and coat thoroughly with the seasoning. Refrigerate the pork, uncovered, for at least 4 hours, ideally overnight.

4. Preheat the smoker for indirect cooking over medium-low heat (250°F, or 121°C). Add some oak or hickory wood chunks or chips to the smoker for more smoke flavor.

5. Place the pork in the smoker. Cook for 1 hour, then spray the pork with the spritz. Cook for 3 to 4 hours more, spraying the pork every 30 minutes, until the internal temperature reaches 165°F (74°C).

recipe continues

6. Pull the pork from the smoker, wrap it in butcher paper, and return the pork to the smoker for 3 to 4 hours until the internal temperature reaches between 203°F and 205°F (95°C and 96°C). When the pork is done, wrap the butts in a towel and place them in a room-temperature cooler to rest for 1 to 2 hours.

7. **To make the sauce**: Preheat the grill or a pit fire for direct cooking over medium-high heat (375°F, or 190.5°C) and place a cast-iron skillet over the heat.

8. Combine all the pineapple teriyaki sauce ingredients in the skillet and stir to blend. Simmer for 5 to 7 minutes until the sauce has reduced by half or is at your desired thickness.

9. **To finish the sandwiches**: Lather the cut side of the buns with butter, and crisp the insides for 30 seconds over a medium-high fire.

10. Remove the bones from the pork and shred the meat. Place a handful of shredded pork on a bun and top with the pineapple teriyaki sauce.

Salty and Sweet: Why It Works in Barbecue

We all have experience with the combination of salty and sweet tastes together. And although there are many taste combinations that create some insanely delicious food, these two tastes together stand out among the rest as a pretty epic combo. So, why does it work in barbecue? Well, the meat and its fat can absorb the saltiness of the seasoning really well. Once you have developed that crust or bark on the outside of the food, you will taste the savoriness and saltiness all at once. This can become a little overpowering! To counteract that powerful taste, we draw on sweetness to mellow it out. This is why we tend to gravitate toward classic sweet barbecue sauces on pulled pork or ribs! We love those salty and sweet tastes together. There are other combinations, like sour and tangy barbecue sauces that do the same thing. But, there is not a lot that's better than salty and sweet. It really is a combination made in heaven!

BACON-WRAPPED BBQ PORK TENDERLOIN

A couple years ago, I started doing bacon weaves as a fun way to cover some of my favorite meats. Naturally, I thought it would make pork tenderloin taste even more amazing with all that bacon fat dripping into the meat making it extra flavorful. This bacon-wrapped barbecued pork tenderloin, savory and sweet at the same time, is the perfection of those weaving experiments. Seasoned with my OTFC All-Purpose BBQ Seasoning, then wrapped in a bacon weave, this recipe will relieve any worries about dry pork. This makes an easy weeknight meal, or a dinner event showstopper. This is what bacon was made for!

PREP TIME: 45 MINUTES | COOK TIME: 2 HOURS 5 MINUTES

Yield: 4 to 6 servings

2 pork tenderloins, trimmed of excess fat and silverskin

2 tablespoons (30 g) Dijon mustard

3 tablespoons (57 g) OTFC All-Purpose BBQ Seasoning (page 38)

4 pounds (1.8 kg) bacon, sliced

1 recipe OTFC Sweet BBQ Sauce (page 43), warmed

SPECIAL GEAR
Butcher twine

1. Lather each tenderloin with 1 tablespoon (15 g) of mustard, then coat each with half of the seasoning. Refrigerate, uncovered, for 15 minutes to rest.

2. **Create a bacon weave:** Place a 2-foot (60 cm) piece of parchment paper on a work surface. Working with half the bacon, start by laying 7 or 8 bacon slices on the parchment parallel to each other. At one end of the bacon slices, weave a single bacon slice perpendicular to the other slices, alternating under and over along the bacon slices. Continue weaving, 1 bacon slice at a time, alternating the weave, until you have a full weave that will cover a pork loin. Repeat with a new piece of parchment and the remaining bacon for a second weave.

3. Place one pork tenderloin at one end of a bacon weave. Use the parchment to help start the roll, wrapping the pork in the weave. Make sure to just use the parchment to start, and not continue with it as you roll, or it will become intertwined in the weave. Repeat with the remaining tenderloin and bacon weave.

4. Truss the bacon-wrapped pork tenderloins with butcher twine to keep everything in place for grilling. Refrigerate, uncovered, for 15 minutes.

5. Preheat the grill for indirect cooking over medium-low heat (250°F, or 121°C). Add some oak or cherrywood chunks or chips to the smoker for more smoke flavor.

recipe continues

6. Place the pork loins on the indirect side of the grill and cook for about 2 hours, or until the internal temperature reaches 140°F (60°C).

7. Pull the pork off the grill and increase the temperature to 350°F (180°F).

8. Return the pork to the grill. Cook for about 3 minutes more until the tenderloins are crispy and the internal temperature reaches 145°F (63°C), basting with the sauce and turning the pork, letting it caramelize on all sides, including the bacon. Remove the pork from the heat and let rest for 5 minutes, before slicing and serving with any remaining sauce on the side.

Do Different Types of Wood Affect Flavor?

When cooking over fire, I have noticed that different types of wood put off unique aromas. So, do these aromas show up as flavor on the meat itself? The answer is: yes and no. When cooking over an open pit fire, without a lid, I have noticed that only really powerful woods (such as mesquite and oak) can carry their flavor into the food itself. If the grill is not enclosed, the smoke the wood gives off will not encompass the meat enough to give it that unique flavor (other than the distinctive smoky flavor).

That said, cooking indirect with different woods on an enclosed grill will definitely create unique flavors! With the lid closed, the meat is immersed in the wood's smoke. You will be able to taste the subtle sweetness of pecan wood or the strong smokiness of hickory.

At the end of the day, do not stress about the different types of wood over an open pit fire. Just make sure to use well-seasoned hardwood, so you can focus on keeping a consistent temperature. If you are cooking on an enclosed grill, experiment with different woods, wood chunks, or wood chips to get that unique flavor.

LOADED CHORIZO SANDWICH WITH CHILEAN-INSPIRED PEBRE

All the choripáns I have tried over the years feature grilled chorizo sausage, chimichurri, and, maybe, some onions. A few years ago, I started substituting chimichurri (potentially sacrilegious, but hear me out) with my own take on Chilean pebre. This tangy, sour sauce has a spiciness I really love on grilled chorizo. Although this loaded chorizo sandwich might be a fusion of many South American cuisines, it is an amazing quick meal you can make over fire. I like to go even further by adding chipotle mayo, but you are more than welcome to leave that out! I hope this delicious sandwich adequately honors its inspiration—the classic choripán.

PREP TIME: 20 MINUTES | MELD TIME: 2 HOURS | COOK TIME: 30 MINUTES

Yield: 6 servings

FOR PEBRE

½ cup (32 g) fresh parsley, chopped

½ cup (90 g) chopped Roma tomato

4 or 5 garlic cloves, chopped

3 tablespoons (45 ml) red wine vinegar

2½ teaspoons chopped serrano pepper

2½ teaspoons chopped scallion, green parts only

FOR CHIPOTLE MAYO

½ cup (115 g) mayonnaise

1½ tablespoons (25 g) pureed chipotle in adobo sauce

Juice of ½ lime

FOR SANDWICH

3 or 4 chorizo sausages, halved lengthwise and splayed open

1 tablespoon (15 ml) canola oil

2 cups (230 g) thinly sliced white onion

2 tablespoons (28 g) unsalted butter

1 tablespoon (15 g) brown sugar

3 slices provolone cheese

1 French baguette, cut into 6-inch (15 cm) segments and halved lengthwise

SPECIAL GEAR

2 cast-iron skillets or 1 large plancha

1. **To make the pebre**: At least 2 hours before cooking, ideally the night before, in a medium bowl, stir together all the pebre ingredients. Cover and refrigerate, so the flavors meld.

2. **To make the chipotle mayo**: In a small bowl, stir together the mayo, chipotle, and lime juice. Refrigerate until needed.

3. **To make the sandwiches**: Preheat the grill for direct cooking over medium-high heat (375°F, or 190.5°C). Place a cast-iron skillet or plancha to one side of the fire 1 to 2 minutes before cooking.

4. Pour the oil into the skillet and add the onion. Cook for 3 to 4 minutes, or until soft. Add the butter and brown sugar to the onion and let caramelize for 8 to 10 minutes.

5. Place a second skillet directly over the heat for 1 minute to preheat.

6. Add the chorizo to the second skillet and cook for 4 minutes per side, or until the internal temperature reaches 160°F (71°C).

7. When the chorizo is almost done, top it with the cheese and let it melt. Remove the skillet from the grill.

8. Quickly toast the baguette segments on the grill, cut-side down, for 1 to 1½ minutes until golden and crispy.

9. **Build your sandwich**: Lather the cut sides of the baguette with chipotle mayo, top with onions, cheese-topped grilled chorizo, and pebre.

SWEET AND SOUR PORK BELLY SKILLET

This is one of my favorite meals to make very quickly for my wife. It is such an easy dinner concept that can be paired with just about any vegetable and some rice. The best thing I love about pork belly is its versatility. You can cure it for bacon, roast it for porchetta, or cube it and make this sweet and sour pork belly skillet. Inspired by Chinese flavors and dishes, this recipe is sure to leave you wanting more!

PREP TIME: 20 MINUTES | COOK TIME: 25 MINUTES

Yield: 4 to 6 servings

FOR SEASONING

1 tablespoon (15 g) kosher salt

1½ teaspoons freshly ground black pepper

1½ teaspoons garlic powder

1 teaspoon red pepper flakes

1 teaspoon ground cinnamon

1 teaspoon ground cloves

½ teaspoon ground star anise

FOR PORK BELLY

2 pounds (908 g) pork belly, cubed

Sliced scallion, green parts only, for garnish

Toasted sesame seeds for garnish

FOR SWEET AND SOUR SAUCE

½ cup (120 ml) pineapple juice

2½ tablespoons (38 ml) soy sauce

2 tablespoons (30 ml) apple cider vinegar

1½ tablespoons (12 g) cornstarch

2 tablespoons (30 ml) water

2 tablespoons (30 g) ketchup

1½ tablespoons (23 g) brown sugar

SPECIAL GEAR

Cast-iron skillet or wok

1. **To make the seasoning**: In a small bowl, stir together all the seasoning ingredients.

2. Preheat the fire for direct cooking over high heat (400°F, or 200°C). Place a cast-iron skillet over the fire 1 minute before cooking to preheat.

3. Place the pork belly in the skillet and sprinkle thoroughly with the seasoning. Cook for 7 to 8 minutes, or until the pork has rendered its fat and the internal temperature reaches at least 165°F (74°C). Pull the pork belly off the fire, remove it from the skillet, and discard the fat.

4. **To make the sweet and sour sauce**: Place the skillet back over the fire. Pour in the pineapple juice, soy sauce, and vinegar and simmer for 2 minutes. In a small bowl, whisk the cornstarch and water to blend, then add the slurry, along with the ketchup and brown sugar, to the sauce. Simmer for 8 to 10 minutes until the sauce begins to thicken.

5. Return the pork belly to the skillet and simmer it in the sauce for 2 to 3 minutes, stirring frequently. Pull the skillet off the heat if it begins to burn.

6. Garnish with the scallion and sesame seeds. Let cool for 3 to 4 minutes before serving.

CHEESY SKEWERED SAUSAGES WITH CARAMELIZED BEER ONIONS

If you follow me on social media, this recipe might look familiar. Yes, the original recipe was chorizo sausage with Monterey Jack cheese and Chilean-inspired pebre. This newer rendition has the same amount of flavor, it just tastes different. The core of this recipe is the sausage. I use mild Italian sausage, but you are welcome to use a spicier sausage. The caramelized onions give us that sweet and bitter flavor all at the same time. The combination of the brown sugar and hoppy beer creates a unique flavor profile that goes really well with the salty sausage.

PREP TIME: 15 MINUTES | COOK TIME: 55 MINUTES

Yield: 4 to 6 servings

FOR CARAMELIZED BEER ONIONS

1½ tablespoons (21 g) unsalted butter

1½ cups (172.5 g) thinly sliced white onion

2 tablespoons (30 g) brown sugar

2 teaspoons kosher salt

2 tablespoons (30 ml) beer (preferably pilsner)

FOR SAUSAGE

10 to 12 Italian sausage links (mild or spicy)

2½ cups (287.5 g) shredded mozzarella cheese

Chopped fresh parsley for garnish

SPECIAL GEAR

Cast-iron skillet, 2-pronged skewer or 2 single skewers

1. Preheat the fire for direct cooking over medium heat (300°F, or 149°C).

2. **To make the caramelized onions**: Place a cast-iron skillet on the fire to preheat and add the butter to melt. Stir in the onion, brown sugar, and salt. Cook the onions slowly, for 20 minutes, stirring occasionally. Pour in the beer to deglaze the skillet, scraping up any browned bits from the bottom, and cook for 10 to 20 minutes more, stirring occasionally, until the onion has browned and is translucent. Remove from the fire.

3. Preheat the grill for direct grilling over medium-high heat (350°F, or 180°C). Leave the grill grate off if you can lay the skewers on the edge of the grill.

4. Using a two-pronged skewer or two single skewers, thread the sausages onto the skewer, stacking them close to each other. Place the skewers on the grill and cook for 4 to 5 minutes per side, or until the juices run clear. About 3 minutes before being done, cover the sausages with the cheese and let it melt. Pull the sausages off the grill and smother with the caramelized onions. Garnish with fresh parsley to serve.

4
CHICKEN + TURKEY

Some people may find chicken and turkey boring. Sure, it can come off as bland, dry, and unappetizing, but that is usually a result of the way it's cooked, not the meat. In my (humble) opinion, chicken is often not cooked to its full potential. Although its inherent flavor is not as powerful as pork or beef, some chicken and turkey can be very flavorful on their own. More often, though, both chicken and turkey need help to make them mouthwateringly irresistible. This takes time and preparation. But when done right, chicken and turkey are just as delicious as other meats.

Chicken tends to have more fat than turkey, which makes it flavorful. Turkey is leaner, but often the meat is more flavorful. And even though chicken might have more fat, it is just as prone to drying out while cooking. As for turkey, we have all tried to power through a dry piece of turkey meat at Thanksgiving. It's never fun. So, how do we amplify these proteins? The keys: brining and marinating, seasoning, and sauce, which may seem obvious, but are all-important for making chicken and turkey truly delicious.

Brining, soaking the meat in water mixed with salt, sugar, and other seasonings, retains the moisture in the meat, keeping it tender, juicy, and flavorful and even helps create an amazing outside crust. I use this technique a lot with chicken and turkey. Marinating is similar to brining except that it utilizes the acidity from citric acid or vinegar to break down the meat to tenderize it, and the marinade itself contributes lots of flavor. Lastly, seasonings like smoked paprika, dried chiles, dried oregano, and cumin add savory notes to help elevate chicken and turkey without making the flavor overpowering. If you utilize all three flavor enhancers, you will see a big improvement in your bird's wow factor.

CHICKEN, TURKEY, AND TASTE

Chicken and turkey are some of the best proteins for fully absorbing the tastes they are paired with. Because neither protein has an inherent overpowering flavor, they can be seasoned with a wide range of ingredients. You can experiment with flavor combinations that would be hard to pull off with more assertive meats. Here are just a few ways chicken pairs with the five major tastes.

Salty

Obviously, salt is essential to any recipe. With chicken, the taste of salt is key to creating a foundation for every other taste to follow. As I said before, brining is an easy way to impart good salinity on chicken or turkey. Soaking in a salt, sugar, and water mixture creates an overall salty flavor on the meat. Another key is to make sure you season underneath the skin with salt.

Sour

Flavorful marinades, with their acidity from citrus, other fruit, and vinegars, can really amplify the taste of chicken. Limes, lemons, and pineapple are some of my favorite fruits to include in a quick marinade as they bring fresh flavor to the meat and help make the chicken or turkey more tender. Another way to add that sour taste is with vinegar. Apple cider vinegar and white wine vinegar create a tanginess that seasoning just cannot achieve.

Bitter

Chicken and turkey pair really well with just about every taste, including bitter. Bitter flavors can be really powerful on chicken and turkey when contributed by the use of beer! I love to marinate chicken wings in beer to bring out that slightly bitter yet sweet taste profile. Another contributor of bitter is greens! Pairing chicken with kale or another slightly bitter vegetable can be delicious as the flavors balance each other.

Sweet

Sweet tastes work best with chicken or turkey either as a glaze or as part of a seasoning mix. A chicken or turkey seasoned to be spicy or very savory is nicely complemented by a honey butter glaze. Sweet on chicken helps reign in the harshness of other tastes. Because chicken and turkey can absorb almost anything you season it with, sometimes you can get a little too much of something, be it savory or sour. Adding a hint of sweetness to a glaze or seasoning can help calm that overpowering one-note taste.

Umami/Savory

Savoriness on chicken and turkey is an essential taste. Because poultry does not have a lot of inherent flavor, using a heavy hand with soy sauce, fish sauce, and even less conventional things like peanut butter in marinades or sauces can take the flavors of these meats to the next level. That said, savory also finds its way to chicken or turkey via fat. Wrapping chicken in bacon or basting turkey in fat can really kick up the savory factor while also making the tastes more complex.

CHICKEN, TURKEY, AND FLAVOR

Other than taste and how it blends with chicken and turkey, pay attention to other sensory details. When you combine aroma, temperature, texture, and experience with taste, you'll realize a wide variety of flavors!

Aroma

Chicken and turkey are relatively simple in flavor compared to beef or wild game, so the aroma you get while cooking it will mostly be of the seasonings, marinades, brines, and sauces you pair with it. That is why some of the most flavorful ingredients can be rubbed or basted onto chicken or

turkey with ease (think chiles, curry, soy sauce, and more). When cooked over fire, the crispy skin of chicken and turkey gives off a distinctive aroma. Once the fat from the skin is rendered and nicely cooked, chicken and turkey take on a pleasantly rich, buttery aroma.

Temperature/Heat

When it comes to chiles and heat, chicken and turkey are versatile. I really love making smoky, rich pastes from dried chiles like chipotles. Marinate chicken breast overnight in this paste and you will have a smoky, spicy treat awaiting the fire. Chicken and turkey also mesh well with fresh chiles when combined with acid and fresh herbs. You get a milder spice level from fresh chiles if you smoke chicken or turkey. If you marinate with fresh chiles and grill the meat, the spiciness of the chiles is more pronounced. That said, fresh chiles also do great work when paired with chicken or turkey in a salsa or chutney.

Texture

Chicken and turkey show a big difference in texture between their white meat and dark meat. The white meat metabolizes less oxygen and iron than dark meat and the iron, along with a few other things, is the reason you see a difference in the meat's color. With cuts like the breast and tenders, white meat tends to be leaner, with less fat. This can make it quicker to cook, but also leaves it prone to overcooking. Dark meat, such as in the thighs and legs, tends to have more fat. These cuts are richer and more tender but they also are more likely to burn on the grill from the fat and heat.

I do have to mention that texture from the chicken and turkey skin is essential. This is where you can get crispy, crunchy goodness, such as on the wings or legs, you just cannot beat it.

Experience

Although chicken does not give us huge jaw-dropping cuts like some we get from beef or pork, I still love it. Chicken is like an old friend you just never tire of being around. Because you can create so many flavors and combine so many tastes with chicken, everyone can find something they like and stick with it. Whether it's smoked and fried chicken wings or grilled chicken breast, chicken has much to offer. As for turkey, it used to be just a holiday meat for me. That has slowly changed over the years, once I realized the broader options turkey offers. Sweet and savory turkey legs are like the best chicken legs you've ever had but way bigger! Don't forget about smoked turkey breast wrapped in a Texas crutch full of butter that will leave you swooning. Turkey has much to offer if you are willing to dig a little deeper for it. Between chicken and turkey, you can create everyday meals that can please just about everyone.

CHICKEN, TURKEY, AND FIRE

When cooking chicken and turkey over the fire, you have to manage your coals very carefully. When cooking directly over the coals, make sure your grill grate is well oiled, as leaner cuts of chicken or turkey tend to stick to the grill if you are not paying attention. Some of my favorite things to grill right over the coals are chicken breasts, wings, and thighs, which all take on fantastic browning from the flames and give off a sweet, slightly bitter character. As for indirect cooking, smoked whole chicken and rotisserie chicken are flat-out delicious. That said, there are not many cuts of chicken I cook directly over the flames the whole time. I have found that chicken and turkey develop deep flavors while staying moist when you cook them using a combination of direct and indirect cooking.

For example, processes like smoking chicken wings to temperature then frying them really help capture that smoke flavor while still getting that crunchy sear on the outside. You can also do it the other way around with chicken that's seasoned to be sweeter. I love to sear off marinated chicken over the flames, then pull the seared chicken to an indirect side to cook until it's done. This technique develops a nice crust, but with a slight bitterness, and prevents the sweet ingredients from burning over direct heat.

SMOKED TEQUILA LIME SPATCHCOCK CHICKEN

If you have never heard of spatchcock chicken, do not be frightened by the name. Spatchcocking chicken (or anything, for that matter) is the process of removing the backbone, which allows you to flatten the chicken, making it "thinner" and eliminating the hollow interior—a primary cause for needing such a long time to cook a whole chicken. Spatchcocking basically cuts cooking time in half. This flavorful, juicy chicken is marinated overnight in a chile and tequila marinade. Smoking it the next day makes it savory, slightly sour, and spicy. Top it with Mexican crema, cilantro, and lime juice and you are ready to go. Don't have Mexican crema? Just thin some sour cream with lime juice for a substitute.

PREP TIME: 45 MINUTES | MARINATE TIME: 4 HOURS | COOK TIME: 2 HOURS

Yield: 4 servings

FOR CHILE PASTE

2 dried chipotle chiles, stemmed and seeded

2 dried ancho chiles, stemmed and seeded

4 garlic cloves, peeled

1½ cups (360 ml) water, plus 2 tablespoons (30 ml)

1 tablespoon (3 g) Mexican oregano

FOR MARINADE

6 tablespoons (90 ml) tequila, blanco, or reposado

8 garlic cloves, finely minced

1 tablespoon (6 g) sliced scallion, green parts only

2 tablespoons (2 g) chopped fresh cilantro

Juice of 4 limes

1 teaspoon freshly ground black pepper

Kosher salt

FOR CHICKEN

1 whole roaster chicken

Mexican crema for garnish

Chopped fresh cilantro for garnish

Lime wedges for serving

SPECIAL GEAR

Dutch oven

1. Preheat the fire for direct cooking over medium-high heat (375°F, or 190.5°C). Place a Dutch oven over the fire for 3 to 4 minutes to preheat.

2. **To make the chile paste**: Place the chiles and garlic in the pot and let char for 30 to 45 seconds per side. Pour 1½ cups (360 ml) of water into the pot and let simmer over the fire for 7 to 8 minutes. Remove the pot from the fire. Remove the chiles and garlic, discard the water, and wipe the pot clean. In a food processor, combine the chiles, garlic, oregano, and remaining 2 tablespoons (30 ml) of water. Blend until completely smooth. Pour the paste into a small bowl.

3. **To make the marinade**: In a small bowl, stir together all the marinade ingredients.

recipe continues

4. **To spatchcock the chicken**: Put the chicken on a work surface with the backbone facing you. Using a very sharp knife, start at the top near the neck and carefully cut along one side of the backbone, while not harming the breast. Once one side of the backbone is free, cut along the opposite side of the backbone until it is completely free. Set the backbone aside to use for stock later. Flip the chicken over and spread it out, so it starts to lay flat. Press down firmly on the chicken breast until you feel a snap. The chicken should lay completely flat and is now spatchcocked.

5. Place the chicken into a large bowl and lather it with the marinade, then rub it all over with the chile paste. Refrigerate the chicken, uncovered, for at least 4 hours, ideally overnight.

6. Preheat the smoker for indirect cooking over medium-high heat (350°F, or 180°C).

7. Remove the chicken from the refrigerator and discard any marinade in the bowl. Place the chicken, breast-side up, in the smoker and cook for 1½ to 2 hours until the internal temperature reaches 165°F (74°C) in all parts of the chicken. Pull the chicken off the heat and let cool for 5 minutes.

8. Garnish the chicken with a drizzle of Mexican crema and fresh cilantro and serve with lime wedges for squeezing.

Brining, Marinating, and Flavor

Marinating and brining are not the same. They are different processes used for different reasons. Here is a quick breakdown that will help you determine which process to use:

Brining: This is the process of submerging a protein in water mixed with salt (and usually sugar plus herbs). Brining helps retain moisture in meats that would otherwise dry out when cooked over fire, like chicken, pork chops, turkey, and some wild game. Brining affords some flexibility for cooking without making food tough. If you're wondering what *dry brining* does, it is a similar process (see page 70) for similar results, but without the water. Both types of brine use salt to retain moisture.

Marinating: This is the process of soaking meat in an acid-based mixture. Marinating is different from brining because it focuses on flavor and tenderness. You can add tons of flavor to protein using marinades containing acid, herbs, and spices. The acid helps break down relatively tough cuts of meat to make them more tender. For both flavor and tenderness, marinating is great for cuts like chicken breasts or thighs. Lastly, be careful as to how long you marinate—anything longer than 2 hours can make poultry tender and mushy.

ROTISSERIE CHICKEN WITH ALABAMA WHITE SAUCE

One of my favorite things to cook over fire is rotisserie chicken. There is something mesmerizing about watching simply seasoned chicken turn into a bubbling caramelized bird over the flames that can make anyone hungry! This recipe begins with a classic chicken seasoning using smoked paprika, garlic powder, thyme, and a few other ingredients. Placing the chicken onto the rotisserie using a three-zone fire, it's cooked until it falls apart. The tender chicken is finished with a drizzle of Alabama white sauce that has a hit of citrus. This delicious meal is also economical as it can feed the whole family!

PREP TIME: 30 MINUTES | BRINE TIME: 3 HOURS | COOK TIME: 2 HOURS 30 MINUTES

Yield: 4 servings

FOR CHICKEN

2 ½ teaspoons smoked paprika

2 teaspoons freshly ground black pepper

2 teaspoons garlic powder

1 teaspoon dried thyme

1 teaspoon dried oregano

1 teaspoon cayenne pepper

Kosher salt

1 whole roaster chicken

2 teaspoons canola oil

Chopped parsley for garnish

FOR ALABAMA WHITE SAUCE

½ cup (115 g) mayonnaise

1½ tablespoons (23 g) Dijon mustard

1 tablespoon (15 ml) apple cider vinegar

1 tablespoon (15 g) spicy prepared horseradish

2 teaspoons soy sauce

1 teaspoon kosher salt

1 teaspoon freshly ground black pepper

1 teaspoon hot sauce

Juice of 1 lemon

SPECIAL GEAR

Butcher twine, rotisserie

1. **To make the chicken:** In a small bowl, stir together the paprika, black pepper, garlic powder, thyme, oregano, cayenne, and salt to taste. Pat the chicken dry with paper towel and lather it lightly with oil. Coat thoroughly on all sides with the seasoning, then refrigerate, uncovered, for 2 to 3 hours.

2. **To make the white sauce:** While the chicken is in the fridge, in a medium bowl, stir together all the sauce ingredients. Cover and refrigerate until needed.

3. Preheat a three-zone fire for rotisserie cooking, with the rotisserie between the two fires, over medium-high heat (350°F, or 180°C).

4. Truss the chicken and secure it onto the rotisserie spike along with supporting grips. Place the chicken over the fire and cook for 2 to 2½ hours until the internal temperature reaches 175°F (79°C). Pull it off the heat and let cool for 5 minutes.

5. Carve the chicken into 8 parts. Drizzle it with the Alabama white sauce, or serve the sauce on the side for dipping, and garnish with fresh parsley.

GOLDEN BBQ STICKY WINGS

If you have never experienced the joy that honey mustard can bring, you need this recipe in your life. After falling in love with some mustard-based barbecue sauces as a child, I learned to appreciate the pairing of sweet and sour with honey mustard. The flavors balance each other very well, and when combined with savory smokiness, they can reach that next level of flavor. These wings are first simply seasoned and smoked then fried for that classic crunchy texture. Lastly, they're tossed in a golden barbecue sauce to create a nice sticky exterior that will melt in your mouth (and your fingers covered in sauce) and have you jumping for joy.

PREP TIME: 15 MINUTES | COOK TIME: 2 HOURS 30 MINUTES

Yield: 4 servings

FOR CHICKEN WINGS

1 tablespoon (7.5 g) chili powder

2 ¼ teaspoons brown sugar

1 ½ teaspoons cayenne pepper

1 ½ teaspoons freshly ground black pepper

1 ½ teaspoons garlic powder

Kosher salt

2 pounds (908 g) chicken wingettes

1 tablespoon (15 ml) canola oil

3 to 4 cups (720 to 960 ml) peanut oil

FOR GOLDEN BBQ SAUCE:

½ cup (120 g) Dijon mustard

¼ cup (60 ml) apple cider vinegar

2 tablespoons (30 g) brown sugar

1 ½ tablespoons (23 ml) hot sauce

2 tablespoons (40 g) honey

2 teaspoons whole-grain mustard

2 teaspoons Worcestershire sauce

1 ½ teaspoons garlic paste

Kosher salt

SPECIAL GEAR

Basting skillet, deep skillet or Dutch oven

1. **To make the chicken**: In a small bowl, stir together the chili powder, brown sugar, cayenne, black pepper, garlic powder, and salt to taste. Lather the chicken wings with canola oil and coat the wings thoroughly with the seasoning. Refrigerate the wings, uncovered, while you prepare the smoker.

2. Preheat the smoker for indirect cooking over medium-low heat (250°F, or 121°C). Add some hickory or cherrywood chunks or chips to the smoker for more smoke flavor.

3. Place the wings in the smoker and cook indirectly with smoke for 2 to 2½ hours until the internal temperature reaches 165°F (74°C).

4. **To make the sauce**: As wings get close to being done, preheat another fire pit or grill for direct cooking over medium-high heat (350°F, or 180°C).

5. In a basting skillet, stir together all the barbecue sauce ingredients and place the skillet over the heat. Bring to a simmer and cook for 10 to 15 minutes, or until thickened. Remove and let cool.

recipe continues

6. **To finish the wings**: Place a large deep skillet over the second fire pit or grill you prepared and carefully pour in the peanut oil. Heat the oil to between 350°F and 375°F (180°C and 190.5°C).

7. Carefully transfer the wings from the smoker to the hot oil and cook for 1 minute. Flip the wings and cook for 1 minute more until crispy, stirring occasionally. Remove and let cool for 2 minutes.

8. Transfer the hot wings to a large bowl, cover with the sauce, and toss to evenly coat.

Double Cooking Wings: The Only Way

For me, there is only one way to cook wings: twice. Now, this might sound strange to some, but double cooking wings is an absolute game changer for making the ultimate chicken wing. There are two ways to do this: smoked and fried or grilled and fried. Both follow a similar process: Smoke or grill the wings until they reach an internal temperature of 165°F (74°C), then fry them until golden brown. This process creates a crispy skin, very tender chicken, and insane flavor. You do end

up cooking the wings past the recommended 165°F (74°C), to more like 170°F to 175°F (77°C to 79°C). Although you might think the wings will be overcooked as a result, they actually come out more tender! And the frying oil captures the smoke flavor from the first cook, which will leave you with an insanely good flavor. This is the only way I will do my wings! You will thank me once you try it.

MAPLE WHISKEY CHICKEN LOLLIPOPS

For all those kids at heart, these maple whiskey chicken lollipops are for you. Though made to look like the candy itself, these lollipops are grown-up in both taste and flavor. The first time I encountered chicken lollipops was at a barbecue festival with some friends. Enamored of how delicious they looked, I went home and made some myself. I have created about half dozen recipes for these lollipops but this is my favorite, by far. You start by removing the bottom section of the chicken legs to make them into drumsticks. My biggest tip is to use paper towels for this—they help grip the meat to get it all off the bone. Seasoned, smoked, and glazed with a simple maple whiskey glaze, these lollipops are epic for tailgating, barbecue nights, or any summer celebration.

PREP TIME: 1 HOUR | COOK TIME: 2 HOURS

Yield: 4 servings

FOR CHICKEN

12 chicken drumsticks

1 cup (114 g) OTFC All-Purpose BBQ Seasoning (page 38; triple the recipe; you'll have some leftover)

FOR MAPLE WHISKEY GLAZE

1½ cups (360 ml) whiskey or bourbon

1 cup (240 g) packed brown sugar

½ cup (160 g) maple syrup

½ teaspoon hot sauce

SPECIAL GEAR

Drumstick hanger (optional)

1. **To make the chicken**: Make a cut about one-third of the way down the drumstick toward the knuckle side. Cut all the way around the drumstick and pull off the excess meat and skin until the bone is clean. Trim off any excess tendons. Press the meat on the drumstick down to form your "lollipop." Repeat this step for each drumstick.

2. Place the seasoning in a medium bowl and, one by one, season each lollipop inside the bowl. Set the drumsticks aside and discard any remaining seasoning.

3. Preheat the smoker for indirect cooking over medium heat (325°F, or 163°C). Add some oak or cherrywood chunks or chips to the smoker for more smoke flavor.

4. Place the chicken lollipops in the smoker, on a drumstick hanger (if using). Cook for 1½ to 2 hours until the internal temperature reaches 175°F (79°C).

5. **To make the glaze**: When the chicken is close to being done, preheat a grill or fire pit for direct cooking over medium heat (300°F, or 149°C).

6. Pour the whiskey into a saucepan and place it over the fire. Bring to a simmer and cook for 1 to 2 minutes. Stir in the remaining glaze ingredients and cook until the glaze is warm and the sugar dissolves.

7. Remove the saucepan from the heat and carefully dip each lollipop into the glaze until it is evenly coated, letting the excess glaze drain back into the pan.

8. Placed the glazed chicken back on the smoker and cook for 5 minutes. Remove and let cool for 2 to 3 minutes. Serve with any extra sauce on the side.

Cooking with Spirits

I love to cook with spirits because they can pack a flavor punch. Not only do spirits enhance the overall flavor of food, they are fun to add to just about anything! They can sometimes feel tricky to execute. Here are a few tips to help make your food top shelf:

- **Avoid cheap spirits:** Although this might seem counterintuitive, use spirits you would actually drink for your cooking. I understand that some of you may have expensive tastes in alcohol, so do not feel pressured to use the really good stuff! Just keep in mind that this ingredient is being used to flavor your food. Use something that is pleasant in taste because that will, ultimately, make your food taste better!

- **Use caution when cooking:** If you did not know it already, alcohol and fire do mix, but not the way you'd like! If not cautious, alcohol and fire can cause major damage with their intense flare-ups. Use caution cooking with alcohol, and avoid pouring alcohol into any cooking vessel while it's over the flames.

- **Let it simmer:** When cooking with spirits, make sure you cook out much of the alcohol, so you are left with just the flavor without the buzz. If too much alcohol is left in the food when cooking, you will clearly taste it—and it's not the most pleasant taste. Simmer the spirits for at least 2 to 3 minutes over medium heat to cook out that unpleasant alcohol flavor.

GARLIC PARMESAN BEER CHICKEN LEG SKEWERS

It might take a few tries to get right, but I've found you can easily and securely keep chicken drumsticks on skewers. Just pay attention to your fire and watch for flare-ups. The chicken legs have a decent amount of fat, so they can burn quickly. My other tip for this recipe is to stay away from super bitter beer, like an IPA or assertive pale ale. Use a lighter beer, like a pilsner or other sweet-tasting lager, for a milder bitterness. Paired with that glorious garlic Parmesan sauce (insane on chicken wings, too) you will be in fire cooking heaven.

PREP TIME: 30 MINUTES | BRINE TIME: 4 HOURS | COOK TIME: 45 MINUTES

Yield: 4 servings

FOR BEER BRINE

3 (12-ounce, or 360 ml) bottles of beer (preferably pilsner or lager)

1½ cups (360 ml) water

2½ tablespoons (38 g) kosher salt

2½ tablespoons (31.25 g) sugar

1 teaspoon hot sauce

FOR CHICKEN

8 to 10 chicken drumsticks

1 tablespoon (10 g) garlic salt

Lemon slices for serving

FOR GARLIC PARMESAN SAUCE

6 tablespoons (¾ stick; 90 ml) melted unsalted butter

3½ tablespoons (22 g) grated Parmesan cheese

1½ tablespoons (15 g) garlic minced

1 tablespoon (4 g) chopped fresh parsley

1½ teaspoons red pepper flakes

SPECIAL GEAR

2 long skewers

1. **To make the brine:** In a large bowl, stir together all the beer brine ingredients until the salt and sugar dissolve.

2. **To make the chicken:** Add the drumsticks to the brine, cover, and refrigerate for at least 4 hours, ideally overnight.

3. The next day, strain the chicken and discard the brine. Pat the chicken dry with paper towel and season lightly with the garlic salt.

4. Thread the drumsticks onto two long skewers, inserting the skewers into the meatier part of the drumsticks, close to the bone for a firm hold, about 1 inch (2.5 cm) apart. Set aside.

5. Preheat the fire for direct cooking over medium-high heat (350°F, or 180°C) with at least 6 to 8 inches (15 to 20 cm) between the coals and where the food will sit.

6. Place the skewers on the grill and cook for 15 to 20 minutes, rotating the skewers every 2 minutes to prevent flare-ups or burning, until the internal temperature reaches 170°F (77°C). If the chicken begins to burn, move it to a cooler side of the grill or move the coals around to lower the temperature. Pull the skewers off the heat and let cool for 2 to 3 minutes.

7. **To make the sauce:** About 10 minutes before the chicken is done, in a medium bowl, stir together all the garlic Parmesan sauce ingredients. Lightly glaze the sauce over the cooling drumsticks.

8. Carefully pull the chicken off the skewers and serve with lemon slices for squeezing.

PINEAPPLE COFFEE–GLAZED CHICKEN THIGHS

If you are like me, then you love yourself some delicious coffee in the morning. With its hint of bitterness, this brewed beverage is more than just a morning wake-up call—I also use it in a few different ways when cooking. In this recipe, freshly brewed coffee adds nutty, earthy flavor to your food and helps balance the sweet notes. Marinated in a pineapple and coffee marinade, these chicken thighs end up sweet and tender. And, don't throw out that marinade—it will make an excellent glaze for topping the chicken.

PREP TIME: 15 MINUTES | MARINATE TIME: 2 HOURS | COOK TIME: 1 HOUR

Yield: 4 servings

FOR MARINADE

1¼ cups (300 ml) pineapple juice

¾ cup (180 ml) freshly brewed coffee

1 tablespoon (15 ml) canola oil

1 tablespoon (14 g) garlic paste

2 teaspoons ginger paste

2 teaspoons sriracha

1 teaspoon tamarind paste

1 teaspoon freshly ground black pepper

Kosher salt

2 tablespoons (40 g) honey

1 tablespoon (8 g) sesame seeds

2 teaspoons red pepper flakes

FOR CHICKEN

6 to 8 boneless, skinless chicken thighs

Chopped fresh cilantro for garnish

Lime wedges for serving

SPECIAL GEAR

Cast-iron skillet

1. **To make the marinade:** In a large zip-top bag or food-safe bowl, thoroughly combine the pineapple juice, coffee, oil, garlic paste, ginger paste, sriracha, tamarind paste, pepper, and salt to taste.

2. **To make the chicken:** Add the chicken to the marinade, seal the bag, turning the chicken to coat it in the marinade, and refrigerate for at least 2 hours, ideally 4 to 8 hours.

3. Preheat the fire for two-zone cooking over medium-high heat (350°F, or 180°C).

4. Remove the chicken from the marinade, reserving the marinade.

5. Place a cast-iron skillet on the hot side of the grill and pour in the marinade. Bring to a boil and cook for 10 to 12 minutes. Stir in the honey, sesame seeds, and red pepper flakes and remove the skillet from the heat. Pour the marinade into a heatproof bowl and set aside.

6. Place chicken on the hot side of the grill and sear for 1 to 2 minutes per side.

7. Move the chicken to the cool side of the grill and cook it for 30 to 45 minutes until the internal temperature reaches 165°F (74°C).

8. About 5 minutes before the chicken is done, baste the chicken with the boiled marinade and continue cooking until done. Remove the chicken and let cool for 5 minutes.

9. Garnish with cilantro and serve with lime wedges for squeezing.

GRILLED CHICKEN BREAST WITH SPICY MANGO SALSA

For me, chicken breast is a bit boring. It's a classic cut, but one that is usually way overcooked. This does not have to describe your chicken breast anymore. This chicken, with its spicy mango salsa, will be tender. It will be flavorful. It will be surprisingly spicy! It all starts with a delicious achiote paste. This amazing blend of Mexican spices (and the crema) can often be found at your local supermarket or online, or your local Mexican market, if you're lucky enough to have one. The flavor is tangy and zesty and one of my favorite things to put on chicken. The two-zone cooking method delivers an amazing crust while also helping control temperature, so the chicken does not dry out or burn.

PREP TIME: 15 MINUTES | MARINATE TIME: 2 HOURS | COOK TIME: 20 MINUTES

Yield: 4 servings

FOR SEASONING PASTE

1 tablespoon (10 g) achiote seasoning

1 tablespoon (15 ml) freshly squeezed lime juice

2 teaspoons ground cumin

1 teaspoon freshly ground black pepper

1 teaspoon garlic powder

1½ tablespoons (23 ml) canola oil

Kosher salt

FOR CHICKEN

4 boneless, skinless chicken breasts

Mexican crema or sour cream for garnish

Lime slices for serving

SPICY MANGO SALSA

½ cup (90 g) diced fresh mango

¼ cup (90 g) diced Roma tomato

3 tablespoons (30 g) diced red onion

1 tablespoon (9 g) diced serrano pepper

1 tablespoon (1 g) chopped fresh cilantro

2 teaspoons diced jalapeño pepper

2 teaspoons white wine vinegar

Juice of 2 large limes

Kosher salt

SPECIAL GEAR

None

1. **To make the seasoning paste**: In a small bowl, stir together all the seasoning paste ingredients.

2. **To make the chicken**: Pat the chicken dry with paper towels, then lather it in the seasoning paste. Refrigerate, uncovered, for 2 hours to marinate, ideally 4 to 8 hours.

3. **To make the salsa**: In a medium bowl, stir together all the spicy mango salsa ingredients. Set aside.

4. **To finish the chicken**: Preheat the fire for two-zone cooking over medium-high heat (350°F, or 180°C).

5. About 10 minutes before cooking, bring the chicken to room temperature.

6. Place the chicken on the hot side of the grill and cook for about 2 minutes. Flip the chicken over and cook for 2 minutes more to create a nice crust. Move the chicken to the cool side of the grill and cook for 8 to 10 more minutes, or until the internal temperature reaches 165°F (74°C). Pull the chicken off the heat and let cool for 5 minutes.

7. Top the chicken with the salsa, drizzle a little Mexican crema on top, and serve with lime slices on the side for squeezing.

EVERYTHING BAGEL SMOKED TURKEY BREAST

While living in Texas, I was surprised to find so much love for smoked turkey. To be honest, before then, turkey was found on my family table only at Thanksgiving (though I also remember eating turkey legs at the local carnival). The point is I had never really appreciated how juicy and delicious turkey can be when you cook it slowly with a gentle smoke. This everything bagel smoked turkey breast is just that. A little ode to my time in Texas, we are switching things up, however, with everything bagel seasoning instead of classic salt, pepper and garlic. Everything bagels are my jam, so I love using that seasoning on just about anything. The slow smoke plus the vinegar–hot sauce spritz will give us a salty, sour, and slightly spicy bite, with the smoke helping retain the moisture. Serve with some classic barbecue sauce or cranberry sauce for extra flair.

PREP TIME: 30 MINUTES | BRINE TIME: 2 HOURS | COOK TIME: 2 HOURS 30 MINUTES

Yield: 6 servings

FOR EVERYTHING BAGEL SEASONING

1 tablespoon (18 g) coarse sea salt

1 tablespoon (8 g) black sesame seeds

1 tablespoon (8 g) white sesame seeds

2 teaspoons dried minced garlic

2 teaspoons dried minced onion

1 teaspoon poppy seeds

FOR SPRITZ

1½ cups (360 ml) apple cider vinegar

1 tablespoon (15 ml) hot sauce

FOR TURKEY

2 whole boneless, skinless turkey breasts

1½ tablespoons (23 ml) canola oil

8 tablespoons (1 stick; 112 g) unsalted butter

SPECIAL GEAR

16-ounce spritz bottle

1. **To make the seasoning**: In a small bowl, stir together all the everything bagel seasoning ingredients.

2. **To make the spritz**: In a 16-ounce (480 ml) spray-top bottle, combine the vinegar and hot sauce. Cover tightly and shake well.

3. **To make the turkey**: Lather the turkey breasts with oil, then coat well with the seasoning. Refrigerate, uncovered, for at least 2 hours, ideally overnight.

4. Preheat the smoker for indirect cooking over medium-low heat (275°F, or 135°C). Add some pecan or cherrywood chunks or chips to the smoker for more smoke flavor.

5. Place the turkeys on the smoker and cook for 1 to 1½ hours until the internal temperature reaches 115°F (46°C), spritzing them every 20 minutes.

6. Grab a 2-foot (60 cm) piece of aluminum foil and place 2 tablespoons (28 g) of butter on it, in the center. Place a turkey breast on the butter and put 2 tablespoons (28 g) of butter on top of the turkey. Wrap the turkey completely in the foil and place it back in the smoker. Repeat with the remaining turkey breast. Continue cooking the turkeys for another 1 hour until their internal temperature reaches 165°F (74°C). Remove the turkey breasts and let rest for 10 minutes before serving.

HONEY HABANERO ROTISSERIE TURKEY LEGS

Honey and habanero make a delicious flavor combination on wings, chicken breasts, and turkey legs. For this recipe, rotisserie-cooked turkey legs are glazed with a honey habanero sauce for a spicy sweet kick. The turkey legs are brined overnight to help keep them moist and create deeper flavor. Seasoned and skewered over the fire, they begin to caramelize. Make sure to wear some gloves when working with the habanero! This is fun to make any time of year, but is a particularly tasty fall meal option.

PREP TIME: 30 MINUTES | MARINATE TIME: 4+ HOURS | COOK TIME: 45 MINUTES

Yield: 4 servings

FOR BRINE

1 gallon (3.8 L) water

½ cup (120 g) kosher salt

½ cup (120 g) packed brown sugar

2 tablespoons (18 g) garlic powder

2 tablespoons (14 g) onion powder

2 cinnamon sticks

FOR TURKEY LEGS

4 whole turkey legs

1 tablespoon (15 ml) canola oil

2½ tablespoons (47.5 g) OTFC All-Purpose BBQ Seasoning (page 38)

FOR HONEY HABANERO SAUCE

4 garlic cloves, peeled

1 habanero pepper, stemmed and seeded

¼ cup (80 g) honey

¼ cup (60 g) ketchup

2 tablespoons (30 ml) apple cider vinegar

2 tablespoons (30 g) brown sugar

Juice of 1 medium lemon

SPECIAL GEAR

Rotisserie

1. **To make the brine**: Preheat a grill for direct cooking over high heat (400°F, or 200°C). Place a large pot over the fire (or on the stovetop), pour in the water, and bring the water to a boil. Add the salt, brown sugar, garlic powder, onion powder, and cinnamon. Cook, stirring, until the salt, sugar, garlic powder, and onion powder dissolve. Remove from the fire and let cool to room temperature. Add ice, if needed, to help cool the water faster.

2. **To make the turkey**: Pat the turkey legs dry with paper towel and submerge them in the cooled brine. Cover and refrigerate for 4 hours, ideally up to 24.

3. Preheat a three-zone fire for rotisserie cooking, with the rotisserie between the two fires, with a consistent temperature of 300°F (149°C).

recipe continues

4. Remove the turkey legs from the brine and discard the brine. Rinse the legs and pat them dry with paper towels. Lather the legs with canola oil and coat with the seasoning.

5. Skewer the turkey legs onto the rotisserie, making sure you are on the thickest part of the leg and close to the bone. Place the rotisserie over the fire and cook for about 40 minutes, or until the internal temperature reaches 165°F (74°C). Watch for flare-ups and spritz the fire with water if needed to cool it down.

6. **To make the honey habanero sauce**: Preheat a grill for direct cooking over medium heat fire 300°F (149°C).

7. While the turkey cooks, put on some food-safe gloves and place the garlic and habanero pepper in a blender. Add a splash of water and blend until smooth. Transfer the mixture to a small saucepan and add the remaining sauce ingredients. Place the pan on the grill and bring to a simmer. Cook for 5 to 7 minutes, or until the sauce is well incorporated and thickened. Pull the pan off the heat.

8. **To finish the turkey**: Once the turkey is cooked, brush the legs all over with the sauce. Cook for about 5 minutes more, so they caramelize, then pull them off the heat and let cool for 5 minutes.

9. Carefully pull the turkey legs off the rotisserie and lather with more sauce, if desired.

SMOKED SPICED WHOLE TURKEY

Seasoned with a holiday-inspired flair, this turkey is juicy, succulent, and—most of all—smoky. The key to this recipe is not overcomplicating things. One major contributor to making a delicious turkey is brining. Although you can do either a wet brine or a dry brine, they both help retain moisture in the bird. Some say wet brining can dilute the flavor and others say dry brining might not retain as much moisture, but I say either can work. Here, I do a classic wet brine to retain the moisture, then amp up the flavor with seasoning. Smoked for 8 hours over gentle heat, the turkey emerges deliciously savory and salty, ready to be sliced. But wait, there is more! A honey butter glaze adds a subtle sweetness and ties everything together. This turkey is definitely a showstopper for a large family dinner.

BRINE TIME: 24 HOURS PLUS 1 HOUR | PREP TIME: 45 MINUTES | COOK TIME: 8 HOURS

Yield: 6 to 8 servings

FOR BRINE
2 gallons (7.6 L) water
1 cup (240 g) kosher salt
1 cup (240 g) packed brown sugar
2 bay leaves

FOR SEASONING
1 tablespoon (8.4 g) smoked paprika
1 tablespoon (9 g) garlic powder
1½ teaspoons freshly ground black pepper
1½ teaspoons ground cinnamon
1 teaspoon ground allspice
1 teaspoon ground cumin
1 teaspoon ground cloves
½ teaspoon cayenne pepper
Kosher salt

FOR TURKEY
1 whole turkey, fully thawed if needed
2 tablespoons (30 ml) canola oil
4 cups (960 ml) chicken stock

FOR HONEY BUTTER GLAZE
¼ cup (80 g) honey
1½ tablespoons (23 ml) melted unsalted butter
2 teaspoons hot sauce

SPECIAL GEAR
Butcher twine, spritz bottle, drip pan

1. **To make the brine**: Preheat a grill for direct cooking over high heat (400°F, or 200°C). Place a large pot over the fire (or on the stovetop), pour in the water, and bring the water to a boil. Add the salt, brown sugar, and bay leaves. Cook, stirring, until the salt and brown sugar dissolve. Remove from the fire and let cool to room temperature. Add ice, if needed, to help cool the water faster.

2. **To make the turkey**: Pat the turkey dry with paper towels and submerge it in the cooled brine. Cover and refrigerate for 24 hours.

3. **To make the seasoning**: In a small bowl, stir together all the seasoning ingredients. Set aside.

4. **To cook with the turkey**: Remove the turkey from the brine. Tuck or clip the wings to prevent burning and tie the legs together with butcher twine. Pat the turkey dry with paper towels, then lather it with the oil and coat thoroughly all over with the seasoning, making sure to get a little under the skin. Refrigerate, uncovered, to brine for 1 hour.

5. Preheat the smoker for indirect cooking over medium-low heat (250°F, or 121°C). Add some apple or cherrywood chunks or chips to the smoker for more smoke flavor.

6. Pour the stock into a spray-top bottle and cover the bottle.

recipe continues

7. Place the turkey in the smoker and set an aluminum drip pan underneath the rack. Smoke the turkey for 7 to 8 hours, or until the internal temperature reaches 165°F (74°C) in the breast. As the turkey smokes, spritz it with the stock every 45 minutes to keep it moist. When the turkey reaches temperature, pull it off the heat and let rest for 45 minutes to 1 hour before slicing and serving.

8. **To make the glaze**: While the turkey rests, in a small bowl, stir together the honey, melted butter, and hot sauce. Drizzle the glaze over the turkey as it rests.

Red Chile Sautéed Kale

This was one of the first recipes my wife and I enjoyed when cooking over the fire. While I focused my time on the meat, my wife made it her mission to get some vegetables into our life. This tender sautéed kale, with its nice kick of spice and slight tang, is a dish we make constantly as a side for just about any cut of meat cooked over the fire, but because of the red wine vinegar and citrus, we really love it with fatty meats, like rib eyes, pork ribs, or pork belly. Just pull the kale leaves off the stems for a tender preparation, or chop them with the stems on, if you like a crunchier texture. Once your skillet is hot, this recipe cooks quickly.

PREP TIME: 10 MINUTES | COOK TIME: 10 MINUTES

Yield: **4 serving**

1 tablespoon (15 ml) canola oil

1½ pounds (681 g) kale, stemmed and chopped

2 tablespoons (30 ml) red wine vinegar

1½ tablespoons (23 g) garlic chili paste

1 tablespoon (10 g) minced garlic

½ teaspoon kosher salt

½ teaspoon freshly ground black pepper

Juice of 1 medium lemon

SPECIAL GEAR
Cast-iron skillet or plancha

1. Preheat the fire for direct cooking over medium-high heat (375°F, or 190.5°C).

2. Pour the oil into a cast-iron skillet and place it over the fire 1 minute before cooking.

3. Add the kale, vinegar, chili paste, garlic, salt, and pepper to the skillet and stir to fully combine. Cook for 5 to 6 minutes until the kale softens and most of the liquid evaporates. Pull the skillet off the heat and let cool for 1 to 2 minutes.

4. Serve with a squeeze of fresh lemon juice.

5
FISH + SEAFOOD

Fish and seafood are fun and rewarding proteins to cook over an open pit fire. Here, you'll find a variety of quick-cooking options that blend well with just about every taste! Some of my favorite dishes, and some of my most popular recipes online, are seafood—probably because they have such a dramatic color change when reacting with the fire, wonderful texture, and are often quick to make.

This category of fish and seafood covers a large range of food. We have freshwater fish like trout. With their delicate texture and a very fast cook, most freshwater fish are tender and pair well with simple ingredients. And we have seafood: think ocean fish such as red snapper, salmon, or tuna. These fish are a little heartier than freshwater fish, carrying a slight brininess from their environment. But they are also very tender. Then there are the crustaceans and mollusks, like lobster, oysters, scallops, and shrimp. Although these fish are slightly different in terms of species, they cook similarly over the fire, with fresh citrus, herbs, butter, and lots of heat.

What unites these different proteins? I have found that almost all fish and seafood are more delicate than beef or pork. This makes the cooking process more intentional. You must be highly aware of preparation, fire temperature, and flavor because the food can be fickle. Letting the food marinate too long can cause it to become overcooked or mushy. Cooking on an ungreased grill or skillet means the meat will stick to it (which is really not fun). Too much seasoning or marinade can overpower the taste of fish and seafood more than other proteins. This is a very versatile category, but it does take some intentionality to do it well.

FISH, SEAFOOD, AND TASTE

When it comes to the five major tastes, there is a fish or seafood to be complemented by each. The biggest key to creating taste with fish and seafood is understanding how much of that taste it can handle before you start to overpower the flavor of the food. These tips should help you navigate those waters.

Salty

Most seafood has a naturally fresh, briny flavor, so adding the right amount of salt can boost it. On the other hand, most freshwater fish are milder in flavor. Both types of fish respond to salt similarly, though. The key to salting fish and seafood is keeping it light. Adding some salt along with other seasonings should help amplify the other tastes in every bite. Be careful not to oversalt the fish, though, as you want their natural flavor to shine brightest.

Sour

Adding sour to fish and seafood can be delightful—if you are careful. Although most seafood and fish do really well with some citric acid or a spritz of white wine vinegar, adding citric acid from fresh lemons or limes before the fish or seafood goes onto the grill can actually start cooking the food before you intend to! Although short marinades of shrimp or fish are delicious, keep it under 20 minutes or your food will become overcooked and mushy. Garnish your seafood with lime or lemon juice at the very end of cooking, so the flavor is fresh and does not mess with the texture of the flesh.

Bitter

Some bitter flavors are easier to pair with fish and seafood than others. I love utilizing grapefruit and the zest of lemons or limes to keep things really fresh. Fish and seafood are easily overpowered by really strong flavors, so bitter coffee might not work as well as it does with beef or pork. Some of the best bitter flavors you can pair with seafood and fish are from fresh greens like arugula, kale, or romaine.

Sweet

Honey, maple syrup, sugar, and just about anything sweet can pair with crustaceans, mollusks, and ocean fish. Sweet glazes do wonders with savory or spice-rubbed seafood. Some agave butter or maple syrup on smoked salmon is out-of-this-world delicious. I love to baste grilled lobster with honey butter to complement its natural umami taste. In general, I try to add a sweet boost to lobster, salmon, and shrimp.

Umami/Savory

I find savory tastes make just about every dish better, including fish and seafood. Adding soy sauce or even fish sauce (doubling down on that fish flavor) to a sauce, marinade, or glaze will help create that delicious umami we all love. I have found that lobster tails, salmon, and shrimp pair really well with savory flavors. However, be careful to not overpower the food with soy, as it can make it very salty and unappetizing (not what you're going for!).

FISH, SEAFOOD, AND FLAVOR

When it comes to painting the whole picture for seafood and fish, we have to look past the inherent or added tastes to the other pieces of the puzzle. There is much that makes these proteins unique.

Aroma

The funny thing about fish and seafood is that the fresher they are the less of an aroma they will have. In fact, if there is a strong "fishy" aroma coming off the meat, then you know quickly it is not ideal for cooking. Once cooking, seafood will have a fresh briny aroma and this should carry through most of the cook. Finished fish and seafood that's not overly seasoned will have a slight savory buttery-ness to the aroma with a hint of sweetness.

Temperature/Heat

Fish and seafood are versatile when it comes to spiciness. For example, heartier fish as well as shrimp pair nicely with dried chiles. Pasilla, chiles de árbol, and chipotles all lend their smoky savoriness perfectly to shrimp and salmon. I love making chile pastes for fish and seafood because the paste creates an amazing crust with delicious flavors. As for fresh chiles, they go really well with lighter, flakier fish, such as scallops and shrimp. I love making spicy jalapeño tomatillo salsa to top pan-seared scallops or shrimp. Adding serranos to a marinade for white fish cranks up the spiciness in a good way.

Texture

We have a wide variety of options for fish and seafood, which means we have a wide variety of textures as well. Still, most seafood is quite delicate compared to other meats even if it is considered "hearty." On the delicate side you have trout and perch. These fish can be flaky, soft to the touch, and fall apart very easily. They carry lots of flavor, but can also be tough to consume because of their tiny bones. Salmon and tilapia represent that nice middle ground, with tender meat that doesn't fall apart quickly. These fish stand up well to longer cooking, like when smoking or making tacos. Heartier fish, such as catfish, grouper, and tuna, are less flakey. They will be firm in texture, but still very tender compared to other proteins.

When it comes to other seafood, mussels and oysters are very soft in texture with a thick brininess around them. Firmer seafood like crab, lobster, and shrimp are slightly soft even after being cooked. That said, they can be rubbery if you overcook them, so be careful.

Experience

Everything about the experience of seafood, for me, revolves around freshness and color. The closer you are to the source of the fish and seafood, the better the flavor will be! Any avid fish and seafood eater will tell you that nothing compares to fish grilled over the flames only hours after being caught. You get the smell of the ocean, river, or lake as well as seeing your food from start to finish. For most of us, there are not a lot of meals we create that follow the whole process from catch/harvest to cook to table anymore.

Another aspect I love about seafood and fish are the colors. I love to watch the drastic change in coloration from the raw to the cooked meat! A perfect example is lobster tails. Most cold-water lobster tails start a blueish-gray color that quickly turns bright red after touching the flames. The translucent lobster meat also turns an opaque white from the high heat. Being able to observe the food while it cooks and see its changing colors is unique to cooking fish and seafood and something other proteins rarely reveal.

FISH, SEAFOOD, AND FIRE

As for the fire, fish and seafood can gain a lot of flavor and flair from the smoke and heat. Most seafood and fish are traditionally cooked over direct heat. It is quick and gives off lots of smokiness to the meat while browning the outside crust for that classic sweet yet bitter taste. The only downfall of direct cooking fish and seafood is that the meat can stick or overcook easily. I grill fish on a well-oiled grill grate or cast-iron skillet to help prevent sticking. Making sure you have enough oil on your grill or skillet will help create that amazing crust as well. Using oil and butter on your cooking surface will also add some umami buttery-ness to the food for a pleasant finish.

When it comes to indirect cooking, there are plenty of benefits for fish and seafood. Getting a nice smoky flavor can enhance just about any seafood protein. The other nice feature about indirect cooking is that you lower the risk of the meat sticking or overcooking. Because you can control the temperature, the skin or flesh of the meat will likely not stick to your smoker's grill grate. This opens up possibilities for taste, such as adding a sweetener! Smoked salmon with a sweet glaze is easy to make and delicious done with the indirect cooking method. Smoked shrimp and smoked lobster are insanely delicious as well. You could even venture into cold smoking salmon for a more in-depth process (but that is a topic for another book!).

Know that when cooking with indirect heat, that lower controlled temperature takes longer to cook the food but affords more protection against burning or sticking for consistent results.

Rediscovering the Taste of Bitter

When most people say a food tastes bitter, they usually mean it is not appealing to the palate. And although most people do not prefer the taste of bitter foods, bitter is essential to our taste! Bitter taste is an amazing palate cleanser, it balances fatty and sweet foods, and is delicious. If you are interested in rediscovering this long-lost taste, here are a few ways you can start. Once you are comfortable, experiment to find new ways to incorporate bitter tastes into your food.

GET REACQUAINTED: The first step to rediscovering the taste of bitter is to identify the taste naturally. While writing this cookbook, I started drinking my coffee black to train my palate to taste that classic bitter taste. Black coffee, very dark chocolate, or young greens are great places to become more acquainted with this taste.

PLAY WITH PAIRINGS: Experiment by pairing bitter with other tastes to complement or mellow the unpleasant bitter flavor. Sweetness and savoriness can really help balance overpowering bitter flavors. Soy sauce or honey can mellow a coffee marinade or a beer sauce. Reducing the sauce or marinade enhances the power of the bitter flavors, so add the bitter flavor toward the end of cooking or you will have a very bitter sauce. You want a hint of bitterness to refresh the palate, but too much is not delicious.

FIND WHAT WORKS: Once you start balancing the bitterness in your food, add young leafy greens to amplify bitter more, or a squeeze of citrus juice. Fresh citrus and bitter food create a tart pairing that boosts the best parts of the bitter taste.

SEARED SCALLOPS WITH BEER PAN SAUCE

Getting those perfectly cooked scallops is all about the preparation. First, pull off that (unpleasant to eat) small side muscle from each scallop. Some scallops might not have the side muscle attached, so no worries. Next, dry brine the scallops in the refrigerator, so the outside surface becomes dry for searing. Do not worry, though, the insides will still be nice and juicy. The key to cooking here is having that dry exterior, so when it hits the hot oiled skillet, that amazing brown crust results! Combined with a salty, herby beer sauce, get ready to have your mind blown.

PREP TIME: 15 MINUTES | BRINE TIME: 3 HOURS | COOK TIME: 15 MINUTES

Yield: 2 servings

FOR SCALLOPS

12 scallops, side muscle removed, patted dry

2 teaspoons fine sea salt

2 teaspoons freshly ground black pepper

2 teaspoons garlic powder

1½ tablespoons (23 g) clarified unsalted butter

2 tablespoons (30 ml) canola oil

FOR BEER PAN SAUCE

1½ teaspoons minced shallot

1½ teaspoons minced garlic

1½ tablespoons (23 ml) clarified unsalted butter

¾ cup (180 ml) beer (preferably pilsner or ale)

2 tablespoons (2 g) chopped fresh cilantro

1½ teaspoons chopped scallion, green parts only

1 teaspoon chopped fresh chives

1 teaspoon red pepper flakes

SPECIAL GEAR

Cast-iron skillet

1. **To make the scallops:** Refrigerate the scallops, uncovered, for 2 to 3 hours.

2. In a small bowl, stir together the salt, pepper, and garlic powder. Season the scallops on all sides and refrigerate again until the fire is ready.

3. Preheat the grill for direct cooking over high heat (425°F, or 218°C).

4. Put the clarified butter into a cast-iron skillet and place it over the heat for 1 to 2 minutes. Add the scallops to the skillet. You should hear an audible sizzle as they hit the hot skillet. Cook for 1 to 1½ minutes per side, letting them sear and caramelize to your desired likeness. Remove the scallops from the skillet and let rest for 2 to 3 minutes.

5. **To make the pan sauce:** Move the skillet away from the fire and add the shallot, garlic and clarified butter to melt. Pour the beer into the skillet, scraping any browned bits from the bottom of the pan, and bring it to a simmer. Cook for 1 to 2 minutes (return the skillet to the fire if you need more heat). Stir in the scallion, chives, and red pepper flakes and simmer for 30 seconds. You should have a nice glaze consistency.

6. To serve, top each scallop with a spoonful of the pan sauce and enjoy!

BAKED LOBSTER WITH BUFFALO CHIVE BUTTER

I am obsessed with fire-baked lobster tails. They not only look insanely good, but also taste insanely good! For this recipe, I recommend grabbing some cold-water tails instead of warm-water because, though smaller, they have a lot more flavor. The warm-water tails (which I cook often) are not as sweet. You want that sweetness to counteract the salty and savory flavors added from the buffalo chive butter. Use kitchen shears to butterfly the tails, which will help preserve the meat underneath for a nice clean look. Just be careful with the shells as they are very sharp.

PREP TIME: 45 MINUTES | COOK TIME: 20 MINUTES

Yield: 4 to 6 servings

FOR LOBSTER

6 lobster tails

1 tablespoon (15 ml) canola oil

1½ teaspoons kosher salt

1½ teaspoons freshly ground black pepper

1½ teaspoons garlic powder

FOR BUFFALO CHIVE BUTTER

½ cup (120 g) clarified unsalted butter

2 tablespoons (30 ml) cayenne-based hot sauce

1 tablespoon (15 ml) white vinegar

1½ teaspoons minced garlic

1½ teaspoons chopped fresh chives

1½ teaspoons Worcestershire sauce

½ teaspoon cayenne pepper

SPECIAL GEAR

Basting skillet

1. **To make the lobster**: Using kitchen shears, working with one tail at a time, cut into the middle of the top of the lobster shell all the way down to the tail. Try to avoid cutting the meat. Once fully cut, use a spoon to go underneath the top of the shell to separate the meat from the shell. Carefully lift the meat up and out of the shell, while still attached at the base of the tail. Lay the meat on top of the shell. Using a knife, make shallow slits lengthwise along the meat.

2. Lather the lobster tails with oil, then season them with salt, pepper, and garlic powder. Set aside.

3. Preheat the smoker for indirect cooking over medium-high heat (375°F, or 190°C). Add some oak or hickory wood chunks or chips to the smoker for more smoke flavor.

4. Place the lobster tails in the smoker and cook indirectly for 15 to 20 minutes. The lobster tails are done when the meat turns from translucent to completely white, or the internal temperature reaches between 135°F and 140°F (57°C and 60°C).

5. **To make the buffalo chive butter**: About 10 minutes before the lobster tails are finished cooking, place a basting skillet in the smoker and add the clarified butter to melt.

6. Slowly stir in the remaining chive butter ingredients, mixing thoroughly with the melted butter. Lightly glaze the outside of the lobster tails with the butter before they come off the smoker, being sure to save some butter for dipping!

7. Pull the lobster from the smoker and let cool for 2 minutes. Pour the leftover butter sauce into a dipping bowl to serve on the side.

LOBSTER TAIL SKEWERS WITH GARLIC TERIYAKI GLAZE

Taking the lobster out of the shell means you can easily skewer the meat for an insanely quick cook, juicy flavor, and fun presentation. The skewers are cooked using the three-zone cooking method on an enclosed grill. This helps keep the lobsters from overcooking because they won't be over direct heat. They will cook quickly, though. Watch for any flare-ups while you glaze the tails. Once coated in flavor, pull the tails off and dive right in!

PREP TIME: 45 MINUTES | COOK TIME: 10 MINUTES

Yield: 4 servings

FOR LOBSTER

8 cold-water lobster tails

1½ tablespoons (23 ml) canola oil

1 tablespoon (18 g) coarse sea salt

1 tablespoon (6 g) freshly ground black pepper

2 teaspoons garlic powder

1½ teaspoons red pepper flakes

Chopped fresh chives for garnish

Lime wedges for serving

FOR GARLIC TERIYAKI GLAZE

¼ cup (60 ml) soy sauce

2 tablespoons (30 g) brown sugar

1½ tablespoons (23 ml) rice wine vinegar

1 tablespoon (15 g) ginger paste

1 tablespoon (14 g) garlic paste

1 tablespoon (15 ml) mirin

2 teaspoons sesame seeds

2 tablespoons (30 ml) water

1 tablespoon (8 g) cornstarch

SPECIAL GEAR

Large skewers, basting skillet

1. **To make the lobster tails:** Working with one tail at a time, use kitchen shears to cut all the way down the spine, stopping right before the tail flap. Flip the lobster over and cut down the middle of the belly to the same point before the tail. From the bottom, cut alongside the tail up to meet the cut on the top of the spine. Repeat on both sides. Gently loosen the meat from the shell and pull off both sides of the shells.

2. In a small bowl, stir together the oil, salt, pepper, garlic powder, and red pepper flakes to make a paste. With a brush, lather all sides of the lobster tails with the seasoning paste.

3. With the lobster tail top side facing you, skewer close to the remaining tail, then fold the lobster over away from you, skewering the top side, adding 3 or 4 lobster tails per skewer.

4. Preheat the grill for three-zone cooking over medium-high heat (350°F, or 180°C).

5. **To make the garlic teriyaki glaze:** Place a basting skillet over the heat and combine the soy sauce, brown sugar, vinegar, ginger and garlic pastes, mirin, and sesame seeds in it, stirring until fully incorporated, then move the skillet to the side. In a small bowl, whisk the water and cornstarch to blend and slowly whisk the slurry into the glaze, whisking until thickened. Set aside.

6. Place the skewers on the grill positioned to sit between the two hot zones. Close the grill lid and cook for 7 to 8 minutes until the lobster meat turns from translucent to opaque white and the internal temperature reaches between 135°F and 140°F (57°C and 60°C). Once they are close to being done, lather the tails with the glaze, watching for flare-ups! Once done, pull the lobsters off the heat and let cool for 2 to 3 minutes.

7. Garnish with fresh chives and serve with the lime wedges for squeezing.

COAL-ROASTED LEMON HERB TROUT

Cooking freshly caught fish over the campfire is one of my favorite memories in recent years. Snagging some fresh rainbow or brook trout, gutting, prepping, and cooking right on the coals delivers some of the most delicious flavors you could hope to taste, and I give you just that with this recipe. The key to cooking these trout is wrapping them tightly with aluminum foil and making a good base of lemons. If you wrap your foil just right, the fish cook quickly while the heat from the coals infuses the trout with the lemon juice and herbs. The result is that powerful zesty sour taste that is so nice on trout. The bed of lemons prevents the trout from burning. By letting the lemons take the brunt of the heat, you do not sacrifice the fish skin or your dinner. Just make sure to keep a nice medium-low heat on the coals.

PREP TIME: 15 MINUTES | COOK TIME: 20 MINUTES

Yield: 4 servings

4 rainbow, brown, or brook trout, cleaned, scaled, and gutted

1 tablespoon (15 ml) canola oil

2½ teaspoons fine sea salt

2 teaspoons freshly ground black pepper

2 teaspoons garlic powder

2 teaspoons paprika

1 teaspoon cayenne pepper

10 medium lemons, sliced

8 fennel sprigs

8 dill sprigs

8 tablespoons (1 stick; 112 g) unsalted butter

SPECIAL GEAR

None

1. Score the outside skin of the trout with 3 or 4 cuts to help speed the cooking. Leave the head on the trout, if desired.

2. In a small bowl, stir together the oil, salt, black pepper, garlic powder, paprika, and cayenne until blended into a paste. Lather the trout, inside and out, with the seasoning paste. Place 2 fennel sprigs and 2 dill sprigs into each trout along with 3 or 4 lemon slices.

3. Place an aluminum foil sheet about 1½ times the length of one fish on a work surface. Arrange 5 or 6 lemon slices in a row on the foil and place the trout on top. Put 2 tablespoons (28 g) of butter inside the trout cavity and tightly wrap the foil around the fish, so it is sealed. Repeat this for all of your trout.

4. Preheat a fire for cooking on the coals over medium heat (300°F, or 149°C) and wait until the flames die out and you're left with hot coals only.

5. Place the fish over the coals with the lemon slices facing the coals. Cook the fish for 15 to 20 minutes until they are flakey and opaque white and reach an internal temperature of 145°F (63°C). Pull the fish off the fire and let cool for 2 to 3 minutes.

MAPLE GRAPEFRUIT BBQ SALMON

The first time I was introduced to grapefruit on salmon was at a winter barbecue dinner. Blown away by the subtle bitterness, I wanted to see how I could expand the recipe with some sweetness from maple syrup and that classic smokiness from the grill. One trick: smoking the salmon on a "plank" of grapefruit slices. Although you could use a wood plank, using grapefruit instead provides subtle grapefruit notes in the smoke, so you get some of its sweetness as well as its noticeable bitterness (do not be afraid of that bitter flavor!). I combine the grapefruit with maple syrup, cinnamon, and brown sugar for a pleasantly sweet barbecue sauce for that final glaze. This is a worthwhile project for those who want to try more over the fire.

PREP TIME: 15 MINUTES | COOK TIME: 1 HOUR 15 MINUTES

Yield: 4 servings

FOR SALMON

1 whole side of salmon, pin bones removed

1 tablespoon (15 ml) canola oil

2 tablespoons (38 g) OTFC All-Purpose BBQ Seasoning (page 38)

3 grapefruits, cut into ¼-inch-thick slices

Chopped fresh parsley for garnish

FOR MAPLE GRAPEFRUIT BBQ SAUCE

2 tablespoons (30 g) ketchup

3½ tablespoons (53 ml) freshly squeezed grapefruit juice

1 tablespoon (6 g) grated grapefruit zest

2½ tablespoons (50 g) maple syrup

1½ tablespoons (23 ml) white vinegar

2 tablespoons (30 g) brown sugar

2 teaspoons hot sauce

1 teaspoon Worcestershire sauce

1 teaspoon ground cinnamon

SPECIAL GEAR

Cast-iron skillet

1. **To make the salmon:** Lather the salmon with the oil and coat thoroughly with the seasoning.

2. Preheat the grill for indirect two-zone cooking over medium-high heat (350°F, or 180°C).

3. Place the grapefruit slices over the heat and sear them for about 1½ minutes per side for a nice char, then move them to the cool side of the grill and arrange them to make a "plank." Place the salmon on the grapefruit. Cook for about 1 hour, or until the internal temperature reaches 135°F (57°C).

4. **To make the barbecue sauce:** About halfway through cooking the salmon, place a cast-iron skillet on the direct heat side of the grill to preheat for the sauce. In the skillet, stir together all the barbecue sauce ingredients. Simmer for 8 to 10 minutes until the sauce reduces by half, or reaches your desired thickness.

5. About 5 minutes before pulling the salmon off the grill, glaze it with the sauce and let it caramelize.

6. Garnish with the charred grapefruit the salmon was cooked on and fresh parsley for serving.

SWEET TOMATILLO GRILLED SALMON

Pairing sweet with sour is one of my favorite things to do with salmon. You accent salmon's fatty savory flavor with a zesty twist while finishing with a light sweetness that keeps you coming back for more. Grilling fish carries with it the fear of it sticking to the grill. My tip is to generously (and I mean GENEROUSLY) oil your grill grates before starting your fire using a good high smoke-point oil, like avocado. I recommend making a double batch of salsa and serving some with chips before dinner. And, if you want to switch things up a bit, add some sour cream or Mexican crema to some of the salsa for a creamier version with plenty of spicy sour kick.

PREP TIME: 20 MINUTES | COOK TIME: 20 MINUTES

Yield: 4 servings

FOR SALMON

1 tablespoon (15 g) kosher salt

2 teaspoons freshly ground black pepper

1 teaspoon garlic powder

1 teaspoon ground cumin

½ teaspoon cayenne pepper

4 salmon fillets, scaled and cleaned

1 tablespoon (15 ml) canola oil, plus more for the grill

Radish slices for garnish

Chopped fresh cilantro for garnish

Agave nectar for serving

FOR SWEET TOMATILLO SALSA

4 tomatillos, husked

1 serrano pepper

¼ red onion

4 garlic cloves, peeled

3½ tablespoons (3.5 g) chopped fresh cilantro

Juice of 3 limes

2 tablespoons (40 g) agave nectar

Kosher salt

SPECIAL GEAR

None

1. Preheat the grill for two-zone fire cooking over medium-high heat (375°F, or 190.5°C).

2. **To make the salmon**: In a small bowl, stir together the salt, black pepper, garlic, cumin and cayenne. Lightly score the skin-side of the salmon, then lather the fillets with oil. Coat the salmon generously on all sides with the seasoning.

3. **To make the sweet tomatillo salsa**: Once the fire is ready, place the tomatillos, serrano, and red onion on the coals to roast for 2 to 3 minutes until charred. Stem and seed the serrano and put it in a blender. Chop the red onion and add it to the blender, along with the charred tomatillos and remaining salsa ingredients. Blend until smooth.

4. **To cook the salmon**: Coat the grill grate generously with oil and place the salmon, skin-side down, on the hot side of the grill. Cook for about 2 minutes until the salmon pulls off the grill grate easily. Place the salmon, skin-side down, on the cool side of the grill for the remainder of the cook, 5 to 7 minutes more, until the internal temperature reaches 145°F (63°C), or is done to your liking. Remove the salmon and let cool for 2 to 3 minutes.

5. Serve with a generous portion of salsa, topped with a salmon fillet. Garnish with radish slices, fresh cilantro, and a light drizzle of agave.

Pesto Asparagus and Tomato Skillet

This is a super quick recipe, especially if you make the pesto before you get to the campsite. Just seal it in an airtight container and refrigerate until you are ready to cook. This complements salmon, of course, but also goes well with chicken and steak.

PREP TIME: 20 MINUTES | COOK TIME: 10 MINUTES

Yield: 2 servings

FOR PESTO

1 cup (35 g) fresh basil leaves

1½ tablespoons (12.75 g) pine nuts

¼ cup (25 g) grated Parmesan cheese

4 garlic cloves, peeled

1 teaspoon red pepper flakes

¼ cup (60 ml) olive oil

FOR SKILLET

1 bunch asparagus, woody ends trimmed, chopped into 1-inch (2.5 cm) pieces

1½ cups (225 g) cherry tomatoes, halved

1½ tablespoons (23 ml) canola oil

1½ tablespoons (15 g) minced garlic

1 teaspoon kosher salt

1 teaspoon freshly ground black pepper

Grated Parmesan cheese for garnish

SPECIAL GEAR

Cast-iron skillet

1. **To make the pesto:** In a food processor, combine the basil and pine nuts. Blend until roughly chopped. Add the Parmesan, garlic, and red pepper flakes and blend until the pesto begins to become smooth.

2. With the processor running, slowly pour in the olive oil, a little at a time, continuing to blend the mixture. If you do not have an open hatch on your processor, add the oil in 3 to 4 batches and process until smooth. Transfer the pesto to a bowl.

3. **To make the skillet:** In a medium bowl, toss the asparagus, tomatoes, and ½ tablespoon of canola oil to coat. Season with the garlic, salt, and pepper and toss again to coat thoroughly and combine. Set aside.

4. Preheat the fire for direct cooking over medium heat (325°F, or 163°C).

5. Pour the remaining 1 tablespoon (15 ml) of canola oil into a cast-iron skillet and place if over the heat for 1 minute before cooking.

6. Add the asparagus and tomatoes to the skillet and sauté for 4 to 5 minutes until softened. Add the pesto to the skillet and sauté for 1 to 2 minutes more. Pull the skillet off the heat and let cool for 1 minute.

7. Garnish your skillet with Parmesan and enjoy!

SMOKED CHIPOTLE MEZCAL SHRIMP

If you are looking for something that doubles down on smokiness, look no further than these smoked chipotle mezcal shrimp. After first seeing my friend Dan Phelps (@learningtosmoke) try these, I had to try myself. Although smoked shrimp might be new to you and you might be scared when you see shrimp cooked for 20 minutes—have no fear. The lower cooking temperature helps keep the shrimp from overcooking. The slowly smoked shrimp develop a nice savory taste from the smoke that gets doubly amplified by the smokiness of the chipotles and the mezcal. Pro tip: taste the marinade to find the spice level you prefer. Chipotles in adobo can be hot, so be careful! This is a delicious dish for almost any occasion.

PREP TIME: 15 MINUTES | MARINATE TIME: 20 MINUTES | COOK TIME: 20 MINUTES

Yield: 4 servings

FOR QUICK MEZCAL MARINADE
¼ cup (60 ml) mezcal

1½ tablespoons (15 g) minced garlic

1½ tablespoons (25 g) chipotles in adobo

Juice of 2 medium limes

Juice of 1 medium navel orange

2 teaspoons ground cumin

2 teaspoons canola oil

Kosher salt

FOR SHRIMP
2 pounds (908 g) shrimp, peeled and deveined

4 to 5 tablespoons (½ stick plus 1 tablespoon; 56 to 70 g) unsalted butter, cubed

Chopped fresh cilantro for garnish

Lime wedges for serving

SPECIAL GEAR
Cast-iron skillet

1. **To make the marinade:** In a food processor, combine all the marinade ingredients and blend until smooth. Transfer to a large bowl.

2. **To make the shrimp:** Add the shrimp to the marinade and mix thoroughly to coat. Cover and refrigerate for 15 to 20 minutes. Do not over marinate.

3. Preheat the smoker for indirect cooking over medium-low heat (275°F, or 135°C). Add some mesquite wood chunks or chips to the smoker for more smoke flavor.

4. Remove the shrimp from the marinade and arrange them in a cast-iron skillet. Discard the marinade. Place the skillet it the smoker and cook for 10 minutes. Scatter the butter cubes around the skillet and cook for 10 minutes more, or until the internal temperature of the shrimp reaches 145°F (63°C).

5. Garnish with fresh cilantro and serve with lime wedges for squeezing.

HONEY SRIRACHA SHRIMP SKEWERS

The combination of sweet, spicy, and sour on these honey sriracha shrimp skewers is one you don't want to miss. The key: do not over marinate the shrimp! Twenty minutes is all they need to absorb as much flavor as possible; anything over the 30-minute mark may mean starting over. If using wooden skewers, soak them in water before use to help the wood stand up to the intense heat from the fire without burning and breaking. Lastly, taste the marinade before adding the shrimp. Add more sriracha for more heat or more honey for more sweetness.

PREP TIME: 20 MINUTES | MARINATE TIME: 20 MINUTES | COOK TIME: 10 MINUTES

Yield: 4 servings

FOR SWEET SRIRACHA MARINADE

4 or 5 garlic cloves, finely minced

2 tablespoons (30 ml) soy sauce

2 tablespoons (30 ml) sriracha

1½ tablespoons (30 g) honey

1½ tablespoons (21 g) tamarind paste

1 tablespoon (15 ml) rice wine vinegar

2 teaspoons canola oil

1 teaspoon kosher salt

1 teaspoon freshly ground black pepper

FOR SHRIMP

1½ pounds (681 g) shrimp, peeled and deveined

Thinly sliced jalapeño peppers for garnish

Thinly sliced Thai chiles for garnish

Chopped scallion, green parts only, for garnish

Honey for drizzling

SPECIAL GEAR

8 to 10 skewers

1. If using wooden skewers, soak them in water for, ideally, 1 hour, or at least 15 minutes.

2. **To make the marinade:** In a large bowl, stir together all the marinade ingredients until blended.

3. **To make the shrimp:** Add the shrimp to the marinade and stir gently to coat. Refrigerate for 20 minutes to marinate.

4. While the shrimp marinates, preheat the grill for direct cooking over high heat (450°F, or 232°C).

5. Remove the shrimp from the marinade. Discard the marinade. Secure 5 or 6 shrimp per skewer, fully flat and stacked on top of each other.

6. Place the skewers on the grill and cook for about 2 minutes per side until the shrimp turn from translucent to an opaque white. Remove and let cool for 2 minutes.

7. Garnish with the jalapeños, Thai chiles, scallion, and a drizzle of honey to serve.

Coal-Roasted Shishito Peppers with Ponzu Dipping Sauce

My wife's favorite thing to cook on the coals is shishito peppers. They are simple and easy to make, and can be done in under 20 minutes! Shishitos are generally mild, but can be really spicy, so be forewarned. To cook them on the coals, I like to use my mesh grilling basket, or you can just cook the peppers right on the coals, but the basket makes the process easier and, I believe, gives the peppers a better char. That said, you will get insane flavors from the coals no matter how you roast the peppers. Pair these salty charred peppers with a savory and tangy ponzu dipping sauce to both mellow the spiciness and accentuate that smokiness from the flames. This is a fun appetizer for any family dinner, or serve as a side with steak, pork, or chicken.

PREP TIME: 10 MINUTES | COOK TIME: 10 MINUTES

Yield: 4 servings

FOR SHISHITOS

8 ounces (225 g) shishito peppers

1 tablespoon (15 ml) canola oil

2 teaspoons kosher salt

1 teaspoon freshly ground black pepper

1 teaspoon garlic powder

FOR PONZU DIPPING SAUCE

2 tablespoons (30 ml) soy sauce

1½ tablespoons (23 ml) ponzu sauce

1 tablespoon (15 ml) rice wine vinegar

1½ teaspoons sesame seeds

1 teaspoon red pepper flakes

1 teaspoon garlic paste

1 teaspoon ginger paste

Juice of 1 medium lemon

SPECIAL GEAR

Grill basket

1. **To make the shishitos:** Wash the peppers with cool water and pat dry. Place the peppers in a large bowl, pour in the oil, and season with salt, pepper, and garlic powder. Stir to coat thoroughly.

2. Preheat the fire for direct cooking on the coals over high heat (400°F, or 200°C). Once the coals are white hot with little to no black, you are ready to cook. Blow off any loose ash from the coals.

3. Transfer the peppers to the grill basket and place the basket over the coals, or cook the peppers directly on the coals. Cook for 30 to 45 seconds per side until the peppers are lightly charred all over. Pull the peppers off the fire and let cool for 2 to 3 minutes.

4. **To make the dipping sauce:** As the peppers cool, in a small bowl, whisk the ponzu sauce ingredients until blended.

5. Serve the coal-roasted peppers with the dipping sauce on the side.

FIRE-CRUSTED OYSTERS KILPATRICK

This is a classic oysters dish from the late 1800s out of San Francisco named after a colonel of the same name. One of the quickest-cooking dishes in this book, either on a grill or pit, these oysters are crazy intense in flavor. You do not need to be an oyster lover to love this dish. You start by loading freshly shucked oysters with cooked pancetta and this amazing sauce. The Kilpatrick sauce is savory with a slight sweetness from the dark beer (I prefer to use a dark Irish beer, but you do you!). A crispy Parmesan-panko crust is the finishing touch. Serve these oysters for a tailgate, as a party appetizer, or whenever you feel like it.

PREP TIME: 20 MINUTES | COOK TIME: 10 MINUTES

Yield: 2 to 4 servings

FOR KILPATRICK SAUCE

¼ cup (38 g) diced pancetta

6 tablespoons (90 ml) dark beer (preferably stout)

2 tablespoons (28 g) unsalted butter

1 tablespoon (10 g) minced garlic

2½ teaspoons hot sauce

2½ teaspoons Worcestershire sauce

FOR CRUST

2 tablespoons (30 ml) melted unsalted butter

2 tablespoons (12.5 g) grated Parmesan cheese

2 tablespoons (6.25 g) panko bread crumbs

FOR OYSTERS

2 cups (520 g) rock salt

8 to 10 oysters, shucked and on the half shell

Chopped fresh chives for garnish

Lemon wedges for serving

SPECIAL GEAR

Cast-iron skillet

1. Preheat the grill or a brick oven for indirect cooking over high heat (450°F, or 232°C). Place a cast-iron skillet over the direct heat side for 1 minute to preheat.

2. **To make the sauce:** Place the pancetta in the skillet and cook for 2 to 3 minutes until crispy and rendered. Remove the pancetta and set aside to cool. Discard the fat in the skillet. Return the skillet to the heat and pour in half the beer to deglaze the skillet, scraping up any browned bits from the bottom. Add the butter to melt and the garlic. Stir in the hot sauce and Worcestershire sauce. Bring to a simmer and cook for 20 seconds. Remove and let cool for 1 minute.

3. **To make the crust:** In a small bowl, stir together the crust ingredients.

4. **To make the oysters:** Place the rock salt in a cast-iron skillet and place the shucked oysters on the half shell on the salt. Top each oyster with a spoonful of sauce, a few pieces of pancetta, and a dollop of the crust mixture. Do not worry if the crust mixture does not cover the entire oyster.

5. Place the skillet on the indirect heat side of the grill and bake the oysters for 2 to 4 minutes until the crust is golden brown. Remove and let cool for 2 to 3 minutes.

6. Serve garnished with fresh chives and lemon wedges on the side for squeezing.

GARLIC-CRUSTED TUNA WITH SPICY AVOCADO SALSA

Seared tuna has slowly turned into one of my favorite dishes (a surprise for those who think I only love beef!). A beautiful crispy crust on the outside with a nice tender center, this garlic-crusted tuna with avocado salsa is the jam. When shopping for tuna, make sure you snag a high-quality fish. Look for sashimi/sushi grade, which means the fish has been prepared correctly and can be eaten raw, if desired. This seared tuna is not cooked through, so the best quality means we can quickly sear it over the fire and the rare fish will be soft and tender. If you are not comfortable with that preparation, cook the tuna to your liking! Whatever you do, slice it against the grain at the end for a more enjoyable bite.

PREP TIME:15 MINUTES | COOK TIME: 10 MINUTE

Yield: 4 servings

FOR SPICY AVOCADO SALSA

2 ripe avocados, diced

2 small Roma tomatoes, diced

1 serrano pepper, diced

¼ red onion, diced

3 tablespoons (3 g) fresh cilantro, finely chopped

Juice of 2 limes

1 teaspoon fine sea salt

FOR TUNA

1 tablespoon (10 g) dried minced garlic

1½ teaspoons white sesame seeds

1 teaspoon red pepper flakes

1 teaspoon panko bread crumbs

½ teaspoon coarse sea salt

3 or 4 sashimi-grade ahi tuna steaks

3½ tablespoons (30 ml) canola oil, divided

Chopped scallion, green parts only, for garnish

SPECIAL GEAR

Cast-iron skillet or plancha

1. **To make the salsa:** In a medium bowl, gently stir together all the salsa ingredients. Set aside.

2. **To make the tuna:** In a small bowl, stir together the garlic, sesame seeds, red pepper flakes, panko, and salt. Lather the tuna steaks with 2 tablespoons (30 ml) of oil, then coat generously on all sides with the seasoning.

3. Preheat the fire for direct cooking over high heat (400°F, or 200°C).

4. Pour the remaining 1½ tablespoons (23 ml) of oil into a cast-iron skillet and place it over the heat for 1 minute.

5. Place the tuna steaks in the skillet and cook for 30 seconds per side. You want to sear the tuna on the outside while leaving the inside raw, or cook the tuna to your desired doneness. Remove and let rest for 1 minute. Slice the tuna steaks against the grain.

6. Serve with a dollop of salsa on top.

6
GAME, LAMB + DUCK

In this chapter, I cover a lot of different proteins. Many of these meats are very tender, share similarities to the big three (beef, chicken, and pork), and can pack a huge flavor punch with different flavor profiles.

Game meat is not only delicious but is also one of the most protein-rich cuts you can eat. Meats such as bison, deer, and elk all carry delicious savory flavor when grilled right over the fire. The key to cooking these meats is overcoming their lack of fat. Many cuts of bison and venison benefit from adding fat during cooking, and other steps to keep it from becoming tough.

Venison is increasingly available across the country, as hunting deer is a popular hobby. Finding local sources of venison, such as from hunters and butchers, might take more dedication than stopping at the grocery store but it is becoming easier. Another relatively easy game meat to source is bison. Finding good ranchers who ethically raise their bison cattle is becoming more common, and this meat provides an amazing alternative to beef. You may even be able to find it in a local grocery store.

Lamb and duck and are both delicious proteins that are easy to find. Lamb is a nice middle ground between game and duck, with a nice fat level and a hearty meat. It can be expensive, but lamb might be some of my favorite meat grilled over fire, period. Duck is the opposite of game meat when you cook it, as it has a distinctively large fat layer on the outside. This is some of the most delicious umami-sweet fat you will ever experience. Though, the fat does make duck unique to cook, as you must pay attention to your fire temperature or you might burn the meat.

GAME, LAMB, DUCK, AND TASTE

Because we are looking at three different proteins, you will notice that the five major tastes might work for some but not as much for others. Game, lamb, and duck all interact with taste differently because of their variation of fat content and inherent flavor. Explore more than the traditional tastes with these meats and you will be rewarded.

Salty

Although these proteins are different from each other, they all respond to salty tastes the same way. Most need to be well seasoned with salt no matter how else you treat them. I've found adding salt to game, lamb, or duck about 45 minutes before cooking greatly helps with retaining moisture in the meat. Salt the meat and refrigerate it, uncovered, for 45 minutes to create a barrier that helps keep the moisture inside. This is especially helpful for meats that don't have a ton of fat, such as game, to help keep them tender and flavorful.

Sour

Utilizing sour flavors on game meat can be done in a couple of ways, but one of my favorites is using red wine. Even though red wine has a slightly sour and sweet taste profile, it can become really delicious when used with bison, deer venison, and elk. Sautéed onions in a red wine reduction carry a fresh, savory, and slightly astringent taste when paired with seared bison. This pairing is delicious and shines when there's a salty

seasoning on the bison. Lamb pairs exceptionally well with sour tastes. Yogurt, red wine vinegar, or lemon juice combined with fresh herbs makes a tasty sauce or marinade for lamb. Many seasonings for lamb are salty and savory as well for that perfect pairing with sour. Duck can benefit from softer sour tastes from vinegar and citric acid, but mostly as finishing sauces. I love to use tamarind paste on duck because it has that slight sweet and sour combination that pairs well with the fattiness of duck.

Bitter

Using coffee as a seasoning or in a spritz helps soften the mineral taste that comes with wild game meat. I love to spritz coffee onto venison as it cooks because it not only counteracts that mineral taste but also helps create a deeper, darker crust. Lamb can be paired easily with bitter tastes from the grill. A nice char on the outside can go a long way on lamb! With duck, I've found it can only be paired with bitter tastes if counteracted with sweetness. Orange marmalade is a great ingredient in a sauce for duck as it combines the orange rind's bitterness and the juice's sweetness at the same time.

Sweet

Sugar and sweet flavors tend to favor fattier cuts of pork or chicken. So, it is no wonder that duck, and specifically duck breast, has a strong affinity toward sweet flavors. Adding a maple syrup or brown sugar sauce to pan-seared duck breast complements the inherent fatty savoriness of the meat. As for game, deer venison lends itself well to more natural sweet flavors from fruits and fruit syrups. Wild fresh raspberries, huckleberries, and blueberries create a nice sweet yet tart glaze for game meats. This sweetness tends to pair well with the mineral flavor of the meat. As for lamb, there are exceptions to this rule, but I find it can only handle very subtle sweet tastes—mostly provided by fresh fruit. Lamb tends to need more salty, savory tastes to amplify its deliciousness.

Umami/Savory

Savory umami tastes pair perfectly with almost all game, lamb, and duck. Cuts of game meat such as bison can be treated similarly to beef, with garlic, soy sauce, and herbs to capture that savoriness. Venison and elk do better with light buttery savory flavors as you do not want to overpower their inherent flavor. Lamb is perfect with savory flavors such as garlic and herbs. Duck does very well with soy-based sauces, but be careful as those sauces can become too salty.

GAME, LAMB, DUCK, AND FLAVOR

When you think about these proteins, there is so much beside their initial taste that needs to be accounted for. As we dive deeper into game, lamb, and duck, you will see that aroma, temperature, texture, and experience play huge roles in completing each dish.

Aroma

Most game and lamb lead with an earthy, grassy aroma. Because most game eats wild food, their meat takes on many of the same properties. The same goes for lamb and it is usually grass finished; therefore, it will be very earthy in aroma. Lamb and game share a similar aroma when being cooked over the fire. They are slightly rich but also prone to charring and the char creates an amazing crust! As for duck, it does not usually have any aroma when raw. As it begins to cook, the duck becomes sweet and rich in smell. The fat rendering over the flames will release a lot of enticing aromas into the air around you.

Temperature/Heat

These proteins all benefit strongly from being paired with dried chiles. A chipotle paste lathered onto lamb or duck is savory and delicious. Duck and lamb have a stronger affinity for dried chiles than game does, however. Game can be paired well with an ancho chile sauce on the side, but the dried peppers' naturally powerful flavors must be tamed to keep them from overpowering the game meat. As for fresh chiles, these proteins all pair nicely with fresh chile sauces. Jalapeño, serrano, and even habanero add a nice bright kick to a chimichurri, gremolata, or pesto.

Texture

The texture of these different proteins has a lot to do with their fat content. The fat on game meat is minimal, which means it has a very lean texture prone to overcooking very quickly. Adding fat to game is key to making it flavorful. Many people like to wrap game meat in bacon, but you can also add fat by basting it with butter or topping it with a rich sauce. As for lamb, this meat has nicely marbled fat but it is more tallow-y than other meats, like beef. This means that the fat never truly hardens and stays greasy even when cold. (This is the main reason serving lamb warm is crucial for a pleasant experience.) Lastly, duck meat has a lot of fat! Duck breast fat is so intense it needs to be rendered first before you can actually cook the meat. When rendered well, duck can have that amazingly crispy crust with an almost beef-like texture inside, and because duck meat is dark, it ends up looking similar to beef steaks as well.

Experience

When it comes to the overall experience of game meat, lamb, and duck, I find they all share one similar quality: adventure! Most people are used to grilling beef, pork, or chicken. If you are looking for some delicious meat but are tired of the same old cuts, game meat, lamb, and duck offer amazing flavors and can be cooked in similar ways to steak. If you love pork for its fat, try duck. It might change your whole opinion on how fat can work when grilling. If you are looking for an accessible flavor profile like chicken that can make everyone happy, lamb can do that! Rack of lamb, lamb ribs, or leg of lamb all bring a light flavor. In the end, these proteins represent exploration for those who are willing to try new things over the fire!

GAME, LAMB, DUCK, AND FIRE

As for the fire, these proteins interact with it differently. Direct cooking and grilling game and lamb develops a delicious crust when these meats are cooked over high heat. Both cook relatively quickly, so be quick to check for temperatures and be ready to pull them off when they are done. As for duck and duck breast, sear it off in a skillet over direct heat, which helps the fat render and not burn as it would when cooking over flames. All in all, these proteins will develop deep, rich smoky flavors from the flames.

With indirect cooking, lamb captures a lot of smoke flavor. Lamb leg, rack, and ribs are great candidates for indirect cooking. Most will need a baste to keep moisture in them. Ribs and leg usually fall apart when smoked for a long time. Whole duck is amazing when cooked indirectly on the rotisserie as it allows the fat to also render well without charring or burning. Many cuts of game meat lend themselves to reverse searing.

When you smoke the meat first to the ideal internal temperature, you have much more control over the ending temperature of the meat. Sear it quickly over the fire and you are sure to convert even more people to cooking with meats like venison.

CAST-IRON BISON RIB EYES WITH CARAMELIZED RED WINE ONIONS

The key to the luscious caramelized red wine onions here is controlling the fire to let them simmer slowly, so they absorb all those savory and sweet flavors from the wine. This takes time, patience, and focus. The bison rib eyes are hearty and delicious, seasoned with a slightly spicy and herbal homemade rub that complements the onions. Cook these rib eyes quickly over the coals, making sure to get a good sear. Since bison is not beef, it's cooked to a different internal temperature—135°F (57°C) for medium-rare. Bison has a deeper red color, so don't be shocked if the steaks look more "rare" than they really are.

PREP TIME: 20 MINUTES | MARINATE TIME: 1 HOUR | COOK TIME: 1 HOUR

Yield: 4 servings

FOR SEASONING

1 tablespoon (18 g) coarse sea salt

1 tablespoon (8.5 g) Szechuan peppercorns, or any peppercorns

2 teaspoons dried minced garlic

1½ teaspoons dried thyme

1 teaspoon dried rosemary

1 teaspoon dried shitake mushroom powder

FOR BISON

3 bison rib eyes

1½ tablespoons (23 ml) canola oil

FOR CARAMELIZED RED WINE ONIONS

1 tablespoon (14 g) unsalted butter

2 pounds (908 g) red onions, thinly sliced

1½ tablespoons (15 g) minced garlic

1½ cups (360 ml) red wine (preferably a drier red)

2½ tablespoons (38 g) brown sugar

1 teaspoon kosher salt

SPECIAL GEAR

Cast-iron skillet

1. **To make the seasoning**: Using a mortar and pestle, crush all the seasoning ingredients into a medium grind, or about the size of kosher salt crystals, or coarser, if you like.

2. **To make the bison**: Lather the bison rib eyes with oil and sprinkle generously with the seasoning. Refrigerate the rib eyes, uncovered, for 1 hour to let the seasoning set on the meat.

3. **To make the caramelized onions**: Preheat a fire for direct cooking over medium-high heat (350°F, or 180°C).

4. Place a cast-iron skillet over the fire and add the butter to melt. Add the onions and garlic to the skillet. Let the onions brown quickly, then pour in the wine and add the brown sugar and salt. Let the red wine boil for 2 to 3 minutes, then cool the fire to around 300°F (149°C). Cook the onions slowly for 30 to 40 minutes, stirring occasionally, until they have browned, are translucent, and all the liquid is gone. Pull them off the fire and warm until ready to serve.

5. Kick up the temperature of your fire to around 375°F (190.5°C) for direct grilling.

6. About 15 minutes before cooking the bison, let the steaks come to room temperature.

7. Place the steaks on the grill and cook for about 3 minutes per side until the internal temperature reaches 135°F (57°C) for medium-rare. Remove and let rest for 5 minutes.

8. Top the steaks with the caramelized onions to serve.

BISON STEAK FRITES WITH SPICY GREMOLATA BUTTER

Instead of the classic steak frites here, I switch things up with delicious bison New York strips and coal-roasted and fried potato frites. This recipe highlights how delicious bison can be, which, although, is very similar to beef, is less fatty and slightly different in color. It is packed with protein and amazing flavor but can sometimes use a little more fat to take it to the next level. That is why we pair it with fried potatoes and herb butter. These two helping hands amp up bison's flavor. As for the potatoes, the key to making this dish amazing is keeping the frying oil hot (while keeping yourself safe). Oil and fire want to mix, so be very careful when doing this over the fire. Grab a deep-dish skillet or Dutch oven to help keep the heat outside. Also, cook only over the coals—not live flame. This will help keep an even temperature and give you peace of mind. In the end, if you make this inside, it will still taste amazing!

PREP TIME: 25 MINUTES, PLUS 2 HOURS TO CHILL | COOK TIME: 45 MINUTES

Yield: 2 servings

FOR SPICY GREMOLATA BUTTER

1 cup (2 sticks, or 224 g) unsalted butter, at room temperature

2 ½ tablespoons (10 g) chopped fresh parsley

1 tablespoon (10 g) minced garlic

1 teaspoon red pepper flakes

1 teaspoon finely diced serrano pepper

Juice of 1 medium lemon

FOR POTATOES

2 whole russet potatoes, well washed

1½ tablespoons (23 ml) canola oil

2½ teaspoons kosher salt, divided

1 teaspoon freshly ground black pepper

4 cups (960 ml) peanut oil or your preferred frying oil

2 tablespoons (12.5 g) grated Parmesan cheese

1½ tablespoons (6 g) finely chopped fresh parsley

FOR BISON STEAK

2 bison New York strip steaks

1 tablespoon (15 ml) canola oil

1 tablespoon (18 g) coarse sea salt

2 teaspoons freshly ground black pepper

2 teaspoons garlic powder

1 teaspoon ground thyme

SPECIAL GEAR

Deep-dish cast-iron skillet or Dutch oven

1. **To make the gremolata butter:** Two to 3 hours before cooking, in a medium bowl, stir together the spicy gremolata butter ingredients. Lay a 12-inch (30 cm)-long piece of plastic wrap or wax paper on your work surface. Transfer the butter mixture to one end of the plastic wrap and carefully roll it into a tight cylinder. Refrigerate until ready to serve.

2. Preheat the fire for direct cooking over medium-high heat (350°F, or 180°C).

3. **To make the potatoes:** Use a fork to poke holes all over the potatoes. Place the potatoes into a large bowl, lather them with canola oil, then season with 1½ teaspoons of kosher salt and the pepper. Mix thoroughly until well coated. Tear off two pieces of aluminum foil, each about double the length of potato, and wrap each potato in a piece of foil. Place the potatoes over the fire, or near the fire's edges, and cook for about 15 minutes, flipping the potatoes every 2 or 3 minutes to cook evenly, or until they start to soften (when you can pinch them

recipe continues

and they have a slight give). Pull the potatoes off the grill and carefully unwrap them. Slice the potatoes into wedges and pat them dry of any excess moisture.

4. Increase the fire's temperature to medium-high (375°F, or 190.5°C) for direct cooking.

5. Pour the peanut oil into a deep-dish cast-iron skillet and carefully place it on the grill. Heat the oil to 375°F (190.5°C).

6. **To make the steaks and finish the potatoes**: While the oil heats, bring the steaks to room temperature. Lather the steaks with canola oil and season with sea salt, pepper, garlic powder, and thyme. Place the steaks on the grill and cook for 2 to 3 minutes per side until they reach an internal temperature of 135°F (57°C) for medium-rare.

7. As the steaks cook, working in batches if needed, carefully add the potato wedges to the hot oil and fry for 2 to 2½ minutes until crispy.

8. Once the steaks are done, pull them off the heat and let rest for about 5 minutes.

9. Once the potatoes are done, transfer them to paper towels to drain. Place the potatoes in a large bowl and add the cheese, parsley, and remaining 1 teaspoon of kosher salt. Toss to coat the potatoes evenly.

10. Serve the whole rib eye topped with gremolata butter, with the fried potatoes on the side.

COFFEE-CRUSTED ELK MEDALLIONS WITH HUCKLEBERRY WINE SAUCE

For those who have not ventured into the world of wild game, elk is a meat you should try at some point. Although much leaner than beef, this insanely beautiful cut of meat can keep up with just about any other red meat on the market. One big key to getting elk as delicious as possible is making sure it's tender. So, I use a coffee marinade on these elk medallions, both to tenderize them and help the flavor pop. Coffee's rich yet slightly bitter flavor pairs nicely with the savory elk and helps mute the "gameyness" that some wild game has—a trick I learned from my friend Brad Prose. I not only marinate the meat in coffee but also use coffee in the seasoning for a nice crust. Top this all off with a slightly savory but lightly sweet huckleberry wine sauce and you've got the gourmet Mountain Man's dinner. If you don't have huckleberries, use blackberries or even blueberries!

MARINATE TIME: 4 HOURS | PREP TIME: 15 MINUTES | COOK TIME: 30 MINUTES

Yield: 4 servings

FOR COFFEE MARINADE

½ cup (120 ml) brewed coffee, cold

2 tablespoons (30 ml) soy sauce

2 tablespoons (30 ml) balsamic vinegar

1 tablespoon (15 g) Dijon mustard

2 teaspoons onion powder

2 teaspoons garlic powder

1 teaspoon red pepper flakes

2 rosemary sprigs

FOR ELK

4 to 6 elk medallions

1 tablespoon (15 ml) canola oil

Rosemary sprigs for garnish

FOR HUCKLEBERRY WINE SAUCE

2 tablespoons (30 ml) red wine (Pinot Noir or Grenache)

¼ cup fresh (37.5 g) huckleberries, or frozen

1½ tablespoons (23 ml) soy sauce

2 teaspoons brown sugar

Kosher salt

FOR COFFEE CRUST

1½ tablespoons (7.5 g) freshly ground dark-roast coffee

1 tablespoon (15 g) brown sugar

2 teaspoons fine sea salt

2 teaspoons garlic powder

½ teaspoon cayenne pepper

SPECIAL GEAR

Cast-iron skillet

1. **To make the coffee marinade:** In a large food-safe bowl or zip-top bag, combine all the marinade ingredients.

2. **To make the elk medallions:** Add the medallions to the marinade, seal the bag, and refrigerate for 4 hours.

3. Preheat the grill for direct cooking over medium-high heat (350°F, or 180°C).

4. **To make the huckleberry sauce:** Place a cast-iron skillet on the grill for 2 minutes to preheat.

5. Carefully pour the wine into the skillet and bring it to a low simmer. Cook for 2 to 3 minutes. Add the huckleberries, soy sauce, and brown sugar and season to taste with salt. Simmer for 7 to 10 minutes until the sauce has nicely thickened. Remove and let cool.

6. Stoke the fire, bringing it to high heat (400°F, or 200°C).

recipe continues

7. **To make the coffee crust**: As the fire builds, in a medium bowl, stir together all the coffee crust ingredients.

8. **To finish the elk**: Remove the medallions from the marinade and discard the marinade. Pat the elk dry, then lather the elk with oil and season thoroughly with the crust mixture. Place the medallions on the grill and cook for 3 minutes per side, or until the internal temperature reaches 120°F (49°C) for medium-rare. Pull the meat off the grill and let rest for 7 minutes.

9. Serve the medallions with a spoonful of huckleberry sauce on top and garnished with a rosemary sprig.

Cooking with Coffee

I am a coffee nerd. I love coffee. Brewed coffee can be bitter, chocolaty, fruity, smoky, and sweet—all depending on where the beans come from, how they are roasted, and the method used to make the coffee. Coffee is an amazing flavor to add to food, but knowing how to do it well will save you some time.

IN SAUCES AND MARINADES: Using coffee in a sauce can help balance different tastes. I like to use mild-flavored coffee, like the classic American brew, because it produces a better flavor on the food without overpowering it. Really strong or dark coffee can be delicious to drink with your food, but it can sometimes overpower all the other flavors. So, combine coffee in sauces or glazes with sweet and savory ingredients, such as balsamic vinegar, orange juice, pineapple juice, and soy sauce. Coffee in marinades can add a whole new complexity of sweet and savory tastes. The nuttiness of brewed coffee does wonders to tone down foods with intense inherent aromas, like goat, mutton, wild game, and more.

IN SEASONINGS: The key to understanding how to use coffee in seasonings is knowing how to grind it and how to pair it with other flavors. The grind size is key—I like a medium grind (the size of kosher salt crystals) because if it's too coarse it will be crunchy and if it's too fine it will be gritty. A medium grind has a nice balance. I love to use chile powders (ancho, chipotle, and guajillo), garlic, onion, smoked paprika, and a little brown sugar in my coffee seasonings. The chiles complement that dark rich coffee flavor with a hint of spiciness and smoke. The other ingredients brighten the seasonings and add a little sugar at the end to sweeten everything.

WILD SAGE AND CRANBERRY VENISON RACK

Since venison is very lean, it will overcook quickly (within minutes) if you are not paying attention. The key to avoiding overcooked meat is checking the internal temperature often and maintaining an even heat with the fire. I tend to cook venison on the rare side to prevent it from being too chewy. I've paired this whole venison rack with a sage and cranberry chutney for a tart, sweet, savory flair.

PREP TIME: 20 MINUTES | BRINE TIME: 1 HOUR | COOK TIME: 1 HOUR 15 MINUTES

Yield: 4 servings

FOR SAGE AND CRANBERRY CHUTNEY

½ cup (50 g) fresh cranberries

¼ cup (50 g) sugar

4 sage sprigs, finely minced

Grated zest of 1 large navel orange

Juice of 1 large navel orange

Juice of 1 medium lemon

2 cups (480 ml) water

FOR WILD GAME RUB

1 tablespoon (8.5 g) black peppercorns

1 tablespoon (8.4 g) smoked paprika

2 teaspoons dried juniper berries

2 teaspoons dried minced garlic

1 teaspoon dried sage

1 teaspoon dried rosemary

1 teaspoon dried thyme

½ teaspoon red pepper flakes

Coarse sea salt

FOR VENISON

1 whole venison rack, frenched

1 tablespoon (15 ml) canola oil

Chopped fresh parsley for garnish

SPECIAL GEAR

Large steel skillet, spice blender or clean coffee grinder

1. Preheat the fire for direct grilling over medium heat (300°F, or 149°C). Place a large steel skillet over the fire for 2 minutes before cooking to preheat.

2. **To make the chutney**: In the skillet, combine all the chutney ingredients, making sure there is enough water to cover the bottom of the skillet. Bring to a low boil and cook for 30 to 40 minutes.

3. As the mixture boils, press down firmly on the cranberries to release their juice and mash them.

Once the chutney is a nice thick consistency, pull it off the heat and set aside.

4. **To make the game rub**: In a spice blender, combine all the rub ingredients and blend into a medium-coarse grind. Transfer the rub to a small bowl.

5. **To make the venison**: Lather the venison rack with oil and thoroughly coat it with the game rub. Refrigerate, uncovered, for 1 hour. Pull the meat out about 30 minutes before cooking to come to room temperature.

6. Preheat the smoker for two-zone indirect cooking over low heat (225°F, or 107°C).

7. Place the venison rack on the cool side of the smoker and cook for 30 to 40 minutes until the internal temperature reaches 120°F (49°C) for medium-rare.

8. Just before the venison is done, preheat a grill for direct cooking over high heat (400°F+, or 200°C+). Pull the venison off the smoker and place it on the grill. Sear each side for 1 to 2 minutes for a nice crust. Remove and let rest for 10 minutes.

9. Slice the rack between the bones. Serve garnished with the chutney and fresh parsley.

SMOKED CURRY LAMB CROWN WITH LEMON MINT YOGURT SAUCE

It has taken me a long time to fall in love with the flavor of curry. As someone who grew up on classic Southern food, curry was not a common flavor in my neck of the woods. With the help of travel and my wife's love for Indian cuisine, I have come to enjoy the subtle delicacy that curry brings to the table. Paired with a savory yet spicy taste profile, I love how well it complements lamb. For this recipe, I make a rack of lamb a little differently, by molding it into a crown. Marinated overnight in curry paste, the rack is scored and bent around an onion (to get a better shape) until it looks like a majestic crown. This presentation is fun and festive for any holiday! The opening of the crown can be filled with stuffing or, as here, cooked jasmine rice. Drizzle the smoky lamb crown with the yogurt sauce for a nice sour kick to rein in all those spices.

PREP TIME: 30 MINUTES | MARINATE TIME: 4 HOURS | COOK TIME: 1 HOUR 30 MINUTES

Yield: 4 servings

FOR LAMB

2 whole racks of lamb, frenched

1 onion, peeled and trimmed

Cooked jasmine rice for serving

Chopped fresh cilantro for garnish

FOR CURRY PASTE

2 serrano peppers, seeded and stemmed

2 tablespoons (28 g) garlic paste

1½ tablespoons (23 g) ginger paste

2 teaspoons curry powder

2 teaspoons fine sea salt

1 teaspoon garam masala

Juice of 1 lemon

1 tablespoon (15 ml) canola oil

FOR LEMON MINT YOGURT SAUCE

½ cup (120 g) plain yogurt

2½ tablespoons (15 g) finely chopped fresh mint

4 garlic cloves, finely minced

Juice of 1 lemon

1 teaspoon cayenne pepper

Kosher salt

SPECIAL GEAR

Butcher twine

1. **To prepare the lamb**: Place one rack of lamb on a work surface with the back of the bones facing you. Find the groove at the knuckle of the bone where you would traditionally slice the rack into single cuts and make a ½-inch (1 cm)-deep cut between each bone at that groove. When the lamb rack is sliced, it should bend easily. Repeat with the remaining rack of lamb and then set aside.

2. **To make the curry paste**: In a blender, combine the curry paste ingredients and blend until smooth. Transfer the paste to a large food-safe bowl or zip-top bag and add both lamb racks. Massage the paste onto the lamb, then refrigerate to marinate for at least 4 hours, ideally 8 to 12 hours.

recipe continues

Wild Game versus Beef

If you are newer to game meat, do not be fooled. Just because game meat looks like beef does not mean it is beef—or should be cooked like beef! Traditional game such as bison, elk, and venison share similar qualities in appearance to beef but, ultimately, need to be treated differently. Let's break it down:

NUTRITION: Although I do not write recipes that are weight-loss friendly, wild game is an amazing source of natural protein and nutrients. Wild game tends to have more protein than beef, less fat, and more vitamins and minerals. If you are looking for a great source of lean meat, add some wild game to your diet!

FAT: The biggest difference between game meat and beef is the fat content. For most meat, the fat is where you get the most flavor. When it comes to very lean and athletic wild game, there is not a lot of fat to work with. Although not necessary for most steaks, the majority of wild game (except possibly duck) requires added fat to make the meat more tender and more flavorful. Wrapping game in bacon or basting it in butter can help make this meat better to eat. Adding fat while cooking is not necessary all the time. Just like with steak, an amazing sauce over elk medallions or bison rib eyes might be just what's needed.

COOKING TIME: Because wild game does not have a lot of fat, it will not take very long to cook. Just like very thin steaks, most wild game can be cooked in 2 to 3 minutes for smaller pieces and 20 to 30 minutes for larger pieces. Be careful not to overcook wild game, though, as it becomes really tough! If you are a fan of medium-well or well-done steak, you might want to avoid wild game. Most game meat should be cooked rare or medium-rare to retain the majority of its flavor and tenderness. Even game cooked to medium can be tough. Whatever you do, try it a couple of ways to find your preferred doneness.

3. **To finish the lamb**: Remove the lamb from the marinade. Discard the marinade. Begin making the crown by placing the whole onion on the cutting board. You don't have to do this, but it helps keep the form better. Surround the onion with the two lamb racks, so the "sliced" sides face out. Bring the racks next to each other to meet end to end, forming a circle, then tie them together with butcher twine, tying the bones on top, where the rib bones and meat come together, and again at the bottom. (You could also tie the twine around the middle of the whole crown.) Set the crown aside.

4. Preheat the grill for indirect cooking over medium-low heat (275°F, or 135°C). Add some wood chunks or chips to the smoker for more smoke flavor.

5. Place the lamb crown onto the cool side of the grill and cook for 1 to 1½ hours until the internal temperature reaches about 135°F (57°C) for medium-rare.

6. **To make the yogurt sauce**: While the lamb cooks, in a small bowl, stir together the lemon mint yogurt sauce ingredients and season to taste with salt.

7. **To serve**: When the crown is done, pull the lamb off the heat and let rest for 5 minutes. Fill the center of the crown with the rice and top that with fresh cilantro. Drizzle the yogurt sauce over and enjoy!

GRILLED LAMB CHOPS WITH ANCHO LEMON VINAIGRETTE

Sometimes, the recipes that appear quite simple can pack the most amazing flavors. These grilled lamb chops with ancho lemon vinaigrette do just that! Lamb chops do not take a long time to cook, so they are great for a quick meal. These lamb chops are seasoned with a savory salt, pepper, and cinnamon blend that amplifies the sour in the vinaigrette. The vinaigrette (which is super *super* easy) is the hardest part about this recipe. Soaking some dried ancho chiles in water to rehydrate them takes the most time. If you cannot find ancho chiles, use chipotles in adobo.

PREP TIME: 20 MINUTES | SOAK TIME: 6 HOURS | COOK TIME: 10 MINUTES

Yield: 4 servings

FOR ANCHO LEMON VINAIGRETTE

3 dried ancho chiles

2½ cups (600 ml) water

¼ cup (60 ml) red wine vinegar

Juice of 1 medium lemon

4 garlic cloves, peeled

2 tablespoons (2 g) chopped fresh cilantro

1 tablespoon (15 g) stoneground mustard

1 tablespoon (20 g) honey

1 teaspoon kosher salt

Olive oil for blending

FOR LAMB

2 whole racks of lamb, frenched and cut into single chops

1 tablespoon (18 g) coarse sea salt

1 tablespoon (6 g) freshly ground black pepper

2 teaspoons ground cumin

2 teaspoons garlic powder

1 teaspoon ground cinnamon

½ teaspoon cayenne pepper

Canola oil for coating the chops

Red radish slices for serving

Chopped fresh cilantro for garnish

SPECIAL GEAR

None

1. **To make the vinaigrette:** In a small bowl, combine the water and chiles, making sure the chiles are weighted down. Let soak to rehydrate for at least 6 hours, ideally overnight.

2. The next day, remove the chiles from the water and remove their stems and seeds. Place the chiles in a blender along with the vinegar, lemon juice, garlic, cilantro, mustard, honey, and salt. Turn on the blender, then slowly pour in the olive oil until you have your ideal consistency. Stop the blender and test the vinaigrette. Transfer to an airtight container and refrigerate until needed.

3. **To make the lamb:** Preheat the grill for direct grilling over high heat (400°F, or 200°C).

4. In a small bowl, stir together the salt, black pepper, cumin, garlic powder, cinnamon, and cayenne.

5. Lather each chop with canola oil and sprinkle with the seasoning. Place the chops over direct heat and cook for about 2 minutes per side until the internal temperature reaches between 130°F and 135°F (54°C and 57°C) for medium-rare. Pull the chops off the grill and let rest for 2 to 3 minutes. As the chops rest, drizzle the vinaigrette over them.

6. Serve garnished with radish slices and fresh cilantro.

HANGING LEG OF LAMB WITH CHIMICHURRI AIOLI

When I started cooking over fire, one of the first things on my bucket list to learn to cook was hanging leg of lamb. This is not a normal way to cook lamb that you see in the United States. Not only is it time-consuming, but it takes diligence and patience to keep the fire at an even temperature without burning the whole leg of lamb. The leg is scored to help the red wine marinade penetrate more deeply, which will help the lamb become more tender. The sour aioli is a fantastic complement to the salty and savory taste of the lamb and adds a creaminess as well. When cooking the lamb, be ready to watch the fire for most of the time, rotating the lamb frequently. The fat on the leg will burn if the fire gets too hot, so grab a cooler of beer and watch that fire diligently. In the end, you will be rewarded with a smoky leg of lamb that is both tender and crispy.

PREP TIME: 30 MINUTES | MARINATE TIME: 4 HOURS | COOK TIME: 4 HOURS 30 MINUTES

Yield: 6 servings

FOR RED WINE MARINADE

2 cups (480 ml) red wine (preferably Malbec)

1 white onion, cubed

2½ tablespoons (45 g) fine sea salt

1 tablespoon (6 g) freshly ground black pepper

8 to 10 garlic cloves, peeled

1 tablespoon (5.6 g) red pepper flakes

2½ teaspoons fresh thyme leaves

2½ teaspoons fresh rosemary leaves

Juice of 3 medium lemons

2½ tablespoons (38 ml) canola oil

FOR LAMB

1 whole bone-in leg of lamb

FOR CHIMICHURRI AIOLI

4 large egg yolks

1 teaspoon ground mustard

Juice of 1 medium lemon

1 cup (240 ml) olive oil

1½ tablespoons (6 g) fresh parsley

1½ tablespoons (23 ml) red wine vinegar

1 tablespoon (10 g) minced garlic

1 teaspoon red pepper flakes

1 teaspoon fine sea salt

1 teaspoon freshly ground black pepper

SPECIAL GEAR

Tripod, butcher's hook

1. **To make the marinade:** In a blender, combine all the marinade ingredients and blend until completely smooth.

2. **To make the lamb:** Score the outside fat layer of the leg of lamb, making 5 or 6 horizontal slits on the lamb, so the marinade will penetrate more deeply into the meat. Place the lamb into a large food-safe container and pour in the marinade. Lather the entire leg with the marinade. Cover and refrigerate to marinate for at least 4 hours, ideally overnight.

3. **To make the aioli:** While the lamb marinates, in a food processor, combine the egg yolks, ground mustard, and lemon juice. Blend on high speed for 30 seconds, then turn the blender to medium speed and slowly pour in the olive oil until the aioli is smooth and creamy. Add the remaining aioli ingredients and blend on high speed for 30 seconds until smooth. Transfer the aioli to a medium bowl and refrigerate until needed.

recipe continues

4. **To finish the lamb**: Preheat the fire for indirect cooking over medium-high heat (350°F, or 180°C). Add wood to maintain a constant temperature throughout the cook, as needed. Position your hanging device (tripod) such that the leg will hang 1½ to 2 feet (45 to 60 cm) away from the fire.

5. About 1 hour before cooking, let the leg of lamb come to room temperature. Discard any excess marinade.

6. Using a butcher's hook, hook the leg through the meaty area of the shank. Secure the leg to your hanging device, bone-side up. Place a large skillet or pot underneath the lamb to catch the drippings. Cook for about 1 hour to brown. Rotate the lamb to cook for another hour to brown. Once fully browned, continue to cook for about 2 hours more, rotating the lamb in 30-minute intervals and basting it with the drippings throughout the cook, until the internal temperature reaches 145°F (63°C). Pull the leg off the fire and let rest for 15 minutes.

7. For serving, slice the leg and drizzle the chimichurri aioli on top.

SMOKED HONEY CIDER LAMB RIBS

If lamb ribs are new to you, you are in for a treat. These delicious ribs fall right off the bone overflowing with savory flavor. Lamb ribs are sometimes hard to come by, so check with your local butcher or order them online. These smoked honey cider lamb ribs are well worth the time—they take about 3½ hours to cook, which is almost half the time you need to cook pork ribs! To test for doneness, the key is not necessarily shooting for an internal temperature, but waiting for the right appearance. When the meat begins to pull away from the bones and you have a nice dark amber color on your crust, you know you are pretty close. If you probe the ribs with a meat thermometer, it should go into the meat with ease. These ribs are a fun quick dinner if you want some smoky savory sweet flair, or a weekend party meal for the whole family.

PREP TIME: 20 MINUTES | COOK TIME: 4 HOURS

Yield: 4 servings

FOR SPRITZ

2 cups (480 ml) apple cider vinegar

2 tablespoons (30 ml) of hot sauce

FOR LAMB RIBS

2 tablespoons (30 g) kosher salt

2 tablespoons (12 g) finely ground black pepper

1 tablespoon (15 g) brown sugar

1 tablespoon (9 g) garlic powder

2½ teaspoons smoked paprika

2 teaspoons ground ginger

4 whole racks of lamb ribs

3 tablespoons (45 g) Dijon mustard

FOR HONEY CIDER BBQ SAUCE

1½ cups (360 ml) apple cider

¼ cup (60 g) ketchup

2½ tablespoons (50 g) honey

1½ tablespoons (23 g) brown sugar

1½ tablespoons (30 g) apple butter

2 teaspoons garlic powder

1½ teaspoons Worcestershire sauce

Kosher salt

SPECIAL GEAR

Spritz bottle, cast-iron skillet

1. Preheat the smoker for indirect cooking over medium-low heat (275°F, or 135°C). Add some apple wood or hickory wood chunks or chips to the smoker for more smoke flavor.

2. **To make the spritz:** In a large spray-top bottle, combine the vinegar and hot sauce. Cover and shake well.

3. **To make the lamb:** In a small bowl, stir together salt, pepper, brown sugar, garlic powder, paprika, and ginger. Pat the lamb ribs dry with paper towel, then lather with the mustard. Sprinkle the lamb ribs thoroughly on all sides with the seasoning. Place the lamb on the smoker and cook for 3 to 3½ hours until the bones have visibly pulled up from the meat and a probe pressed into the meat goes in very easily. Spritz the lamb with the vinegar mixture about every 30 minutes

recipe continues

4. **To make the sauce**: As the lamb smokes, preheat a grill for direct cooking over medium-high heat (375°F, or 190.5°C). Place a cast-iron skillet over the fire.

5. Pour in the apple cider and let cook for 2 to 3 minutes until reduced by half. Add the remaining sauce ingredients and cook for 7 to 8 minutes, stirring, until thickened. Pull the sauce off the heat and let cool. Lather the lamb ribs with the barbecue sauce about 15 minutes before they will be pulled off the smoker. Remove and let cool for 5 minutes.

Beer + Food + Flavor

Lots of people love drinking beer! But did you know you can use it in your cooking? From marinating to deglazing, beer can be used in many ways, including as a complement to the food itself. Here is a quick breakdown of four different types of common beer flavors, beer styles, and how they can be used to enhance your foods:

Crisp

STYLES: Amber lagers, pilsners, and wheat beers
FLAVOR: Refreshing, bright and clean
USES/PAIRINGS: Great for marinating, brining, or spritzing, because the flavor is light and not overly powerful. Pairs well with chicken and seafood.

Malt

STYLES: Dunkel, ESB (extra special bitter), and Scottish ales
FLAVOR: Slightly sweet and nutty
USES/PAIRINGS: Fantastic for making barbecue sauce, glazes, and spritzes. Pairs well with barbecue, burgers, and meat in general.

Hoppy

STYLES: Amber ales, IPAs, and pale ales
FLAVOR: Bitter, sometimes fruity and sharp
USES/PAIRINGS: Great flavor to glaze for adding a subtle bitterness. Pairs well with pork, spicy foods, and steak.

Dark

STYLES: Brown ales, porters, and stouts
FLAVOR: Dark, subtly sweet with a bitter aftertaste
USES/PAIRINGS: Great for deglazing, injecting, and in sauces. Pairs well with barbecue, pork, and steak.

SEARED DUCK BREAST WITH BLACK CHERRY TAMARIND SAUCE

Making perfectly seared duck breast over the fire can be out-of-this-world tasty, but it does take a bit of knowledge. Duck breast has this amazingly delicious fat layer on one side that can make any dish delicious (Duck fat fries anyone?). The key to cooking duck is getting that fat to render well. Start with the duck breast in a cold skillet. This helps get an even sear on the breast and prevents burning. Placing that skillet over a medium-low heat gives you that golden brown crust by cooking low and slow. If the sides begin to curl or the fat bows in the middle, place a smaller cast-iron skillet on top of the breast to flatten it. Another thing that can blow people's minds is that we cook the duck to 130°F (54°C) for medium-rare. I know, you probably think I am crazy since duck is a bird and most birds (like chicken) require a lot higher internal temperature. Duck is different! It can be eaten at lower temperatures. Top that perfectly seared and cooked duck with a sweet and sour black cherry tamarind sauce for the win!

PREP TIME: 15 MINUTES | COOK TIME: 40 MINUTES

Yield: 2 servings

FOR DUCK BREAST

2 whole star anise

2 teaspoons coarse sea salt

1 teaspoon fennel seeds

½ teaspoon Szechuan peppercorns

½ teaspoon ground cinnamon

¼ teaspoon ground cloves

3 duck breasts

Toasted sesame seeds for garnish

FOR BLACK CHERRY TAMARIND SAUCE

2 tablespoons (30 ml) red wine

1 tablespoon (14 g) unsalted butter

4 garlic cloves, minced

2 teaspoons ginger paste

1½ tablespoons (23 ml) soy sauce

1½ tablespoons (21 g) tamarind paste

1 tablespoon (15 ml) apple cider vinegar

1 tablespoon (20 g) honey

¼ cup (40 g) black cherries, stemmed, pitted, and minced

SPECIAL GEAR

Large cast-iron skillet

1. **To make the duck**: In a spice grinder or clean coffee grinder, combine the star anise, salt, and fennel seeds. Grind until the spices are a fine grain. Transfer to a small bowl and stir in the cinnamon and cloves.

2. Score the duck on the fat side using a crosshatch pattern with ⅛ inch (0.03 cm) between each score. Make sure to score evenly and not too deeply (you do not want to score the meat below the fat). Coat the duck on all sides with the seasoning and place it into a large, cold cast-iron skillet.

3. Preheat the grill for direct cooking over medium heat (325°F, or 163°C).

4. Place the skillet with the duck breast over the flames and begin letting the duck breast crisp. Cook the duck like this for 15 to 18 minutes until you have a golden-brown sear on all sides of the fat. Stoke your fire a little to get it hotter, then flip the breasts over to cook, flesh-side down, for 3 to 5 minutes

more. Cook the duck until it reaches an internal temperature of 130°F (54°C) for medium-rare. Pull the duck off the heat and out of the skillet and let rest for 10 minutes.

5. **To make the black cherry sauce**: While the duck rests, return the skillet to the grill and pour in the red wine to deglaze it, scraping up any browned bits from the bottom. Add the butter, garlic, and ginger paste. Simmer for 1 to 2 minutes, then stir in the remaining sauce ingredients. Let the sauce simmer over medium heat for about 10 minutes until thickened, stirring occasionally. Pull the sauce off the heat.

6. Slice the duck breast at a slight angle, drizzle the sauce over the top, and garnish with toasted sesame seeds.

SPICY HOISIN JERK ROTISSERIE DUCK

This dish combines myriad flavors—a spicy, savory-yet-sweet hoisin glaze will be the first thing you taste, followed by a salty, spicy, herbal jerk seasoning that brings a little more kick to this dish. Finally, the duck meat and that fat will shine through giving you a perfectly sweet, salty, and slightly savory bite. The key to cooking duck on the rotisserie is scoring the fat on the breast to help the fat render and, ultimately, make the food more flavorful. Note that you'll need a rotisserie and butcher twine for this recipe.

PREP TIME: 25 MINUTES | BRINE TIME: 4 HOURS | COOK TIME: 2 HOURS 30 MINUTES

Yield: 4 servings

FOR JERK SEASONING

1 tablespoon (9 g) garlic powder

2 teaspoons smoked paprika

2 teaspoons cayenne pepper

1½ teaspoons onion powder

1½ teaspoons brown sugar

1½ teaspoons fine sea salt

1 teaspoon freshly ground black pepper

1 teaspoon ground thyme

1 teaspoon ground cinnamon

½ teaspoon ground allspice

½ teaspoon ground ginger

FOR DUCK

1 whole duck, giblets and neck removed

1 tablespoon (15 ml) canola oil

FOR SPICY HOISIN GLAZE

¼ cup (60 ml) soy sauce

2½ tablespoons (40 g) creamy peanut butter

1 tablespoon (15 ml) rice wine vinegar

1 tablespoon (15 ml) sriracha

1½ teaspoons honey

1½ teaspoons garlic paste

1 teaspoon sesame oil

1 teaspoon miso paste or black bean paste

1. **To make the jerk seasoning**: In a small bowl, stir together all the jerk seasoning ingredients.

2. **To make the duck**: Grab the duck and pat it dry with paper towels. Cut a length of butcher twine about 2½ times the size of the duck. Soak the twine in water for 10 minutes. Remove the twine from the water and carefully truss the duck for the rotisserie. Gently score the outside of the duck breast skin, so the fat can render. Make 4 equal-size slits horizontally on each breasts. Lather the duck with oil and coat the duck generously all over with the jerk seasoning. Refrigerate, uncovered, for at least 4 hours, ideally overnight.

3. Preheat a three-zone fire in your covered grill for rotisserie cooking, with the rotisserie between the two fires, over medium-high heat (350°F, or 180°C).

4. Let the duck come to room temperature about 1 hour before cooking.

5. Place the duck on the skewer and secure the prongs. Place the duck over the middle, cooler, part of the fire and put an aluminum foil pan filled with water under it to prevent flare-ups. Cook the duck for 1½ to 2 hours until the duck reaches and internal temperature of about 180°F (82°C).

6. **To make the spicy hoisin glaze**: As the duck cooks, in a small bowl, stir together all the glaze ingredients.

7. About 30 minutes before the duck is done, glaze the outside of the duck every 10 minutes with the glaze until done. Pull the duck off the heat and let it cool for 10 minutes.

8. Pull the duck off the rotisserie and remove the butcher twine. Carve the duck to serve.

RESOURCES
GEAR, MATERIALS, AND MORE

Spices and Meat
Porter Road Butcher (PorterRoad.com)

Chris and James created Porter Road Butcher in my hometown (Nashville, Tennessee) awhile back. What started as a local butcher shop dedicated to providing high-quality local meat has turned into an online meat empire. These two are now able to ship their amazing products all over the country, including my favorite picanha. Although they are now a larger business, I still love shopping at their store in East Nashville.

RECOMMENDED: PICANHA, HANGER STEAK, AND FLAP STEAK

Spiceology + Derek Wolf (Spiceology.com)

For years, I have had the pleasure of creating different lines of seasonings and rubs with Spiceology. Inspired by everything from my travels to flavors that stand out from my childhood to my current passions, the team at Spiceology helped me create lines like American Inspired, beer-infused BBQ rubs (in beer cans!), and spirit-infused rubs. If you love my recipes, these spices are an amazing next step to tempt your taste buds!

RECOMMENDED: CHIPOTLE GARLIC BBQ RUB, GAUCHO STEAKHOUSE RUB, AND HICKORY PEACH PORTER RUB

Grills, Skillets, and Wood
Breeo (Breeo.co)

Breeo is a brand of American-made smokeless grill I have been using for years. It creates an amazing cooking experience that provides consistent heat for all direct styles of fire cooking. This has been my daily grill for a while!

RECOMMENDED: X SERIES AND THE OUTPOST

Cowboy Charcoal (CowboyCharcoal.com)

The team at Cowboy Charcoal/Western BBQ Wood/ Duraflame are on a mission to make quality charcoal and wood affordable. I love their lump charcoal because it is so easy to light, keeps a lasting heat, and creates an amazing aroma. Pairing it with some of their wood chips or wood chunks is just the cherry on top of a great cook.

RECOMMENDED: OAK AND HICKORY NATURAL LUMP CHARCOAL AND THE MESQUITE WOOD CHIPS

Kankay Amara (KankayTexas.com)

This little South American–based grilling company makes some simple and approachable fire cooking devices. I have fallen in love with how easy they are to light, as well as the variety of cooking styles you can try on them.

RECOMMENDED: KANKAY AMARA GRILL 2.0

Lodge Cast Iron (LodgeCastIron.com)

If you are looking for a variety of cast-iron products as well as fire cooking gear, look no further than Lodge Cast Iron. With their foundry only a short distance from where I live, they are a local Tennessee business with a large following. I used their cast-iron skillets, basting skillet, basting brush, and tri-pod while making this cookbook. Look through their site, and you will find many fun cooking apparatuses to try.

RECOMMENDED: 12-INCH (30 CM) CAST-IRON SKILLET, DUTCH OVEN TRI-POD, AND MELTING SKILLET

Oklahoma Joe's Smokers (OklahomaJoes.com)

If you are looking for a top-notch smoker, look no further than Oklahoma Joe's. They have many options for smokers you can use for both direct and indirect styles of fire cooking. They also have a starter smoker for those just venturing into barbecue.

RECOMMENDED: HIGHLAND AND THE BRONCO

Specialty Fire Cooking Equipment
Kanka Grill (KankaGrill.com)

This is an excellent rotisserie you can use with just about any grill, and it can handle large amounts of weight.

RECOMMENDED: THE KANKA GRILL ROTISSERIE

Super Skewer (SuperSkewer.com)

These are the only skewers I use to cook over the fire. They are high quality, large enough to handle a lot of meat, and easy to clean.

RECOMMENDED: BRAZILIAN CHURRASCO SKEWER AND FORKED SKEWER

Knives and Cutting Boards
Fingal Ferguson (FingalFergusonKnives.com)

The mad Irishman behind my favorite knives is none other than Fingal Ferguson. He makes some of the most beautiful knives on the planet. I highly recommend grabbing some (if you can find one before it sells out)!

RECOMMENDED: ANYTHING!

Monnier Woodcraft (MonnierWoodcraft.com)

Monnier Woodcraft cutting boards have been the only cutting boards I have used for years. They are durable and extremely high quality. Made in Texas, buying one also means supporting American artists.

RECOMMENDED: ANY END-GRAIN CUTTING BOARD

ACKNOWLEDGMENTS

For those who do not know, running Over The Fire Cooking is a huge team effort. It is not just me, but many people who make this all happen!

First off to my wife, Ally, I love you more than you could ever know. You have stuck with me through thick and thin (especially around this business). You are the real CEO, decision maker, and more. Thank you for always making each day a joy. I love you.

To my family, thank you so much for always helping and volunteering to eat my leftovers! To my parents, Brad and Denise, you have given me such an amazing vision and drive for life. You were the ones who helped start all of this, and still find time in your busy lives to help. I love you. To Jenna, Evan, and Skye, thank you for always encouraging, leading first, and speaking honesty to me and this business. You are my role models! To the whole Klinker Family, you are the perfect blend of love with a hint of crazy. You have always shown me not to run away from new things, embrace being uncomfortable, and thoroughly enjoy it when things work out. Thank you.

To the OTFC team, y'all rock! To Kita, don't ever stop pushing us for more and better. You always keep us on track and give way more than is required. Thank you! To Brad and Jeremy, thank you for so many long phone calls chatting about recipes, ideas, and more. You two will always have more cooking knowledge than I, and I'm glad to have you on the team.

To all our Friends, thank you for always saying "yes" to helping or volunteering. To Drew, Erin, Anthony, Haley, Mitchell, Rebecca, Josiah, and Victoria—so many things for this cookbook would not have happened if it wasn't for all of your help. Thank you so much.

And lastly to my Followers and Fans, you are the bedrock of all of this. You fill me with excitement every day seeing photos, videos, comments, and likes around our recipes. You watch, engage, and enjoy our content with such enthusiasm. Thank you for making this all happen. We would not be here without you!

To anyone I forgot, thank you so much! We are truly humbled to have another cookbook, and excited to see what the future holds!

ABOUT THE AUTHOR

Derek Wolf is the man behind Over The Fire Cooking: a website, video, and social media phenomenon dedicated to bringing fire, food, and people together. Derek, along with his wife, Ally, frequently travels around the world to learn new techniques and recipes, works with various brands, from Cowboy Charcoal to Oklahoma Joe's, and has multiple bestselling spice lines with Spiceology.

With his first book, Food by Fire, hitting the stage in 2020, he has been featured everywhere from Forbes to Men's Health, made TV shorts with Buffalo Trace, and loves cooking for large crowds at festivals. In addition to his original recipes and videos, Derek builds community on his pages by featuring the adventures of other fire-cooking enthusiasts who inspire him. Most weeks, you can still find him working on new recipes, then producing and showcasing them on his website and socials.

Check out more of Derek's work on Instagram, Facebook, YouTube, and more at @OverTheFireCooking, or visit him at OverTheFireCooking.com.

INDEX